Speech Rights in America

THE HISTORY OF COMMUNICATION

Robert W. McChesney
and John C. Nerone, editors

*A list of books in the series
appears at the end of this book.*

Speech Rights in America

THE FIRST AMENDMENT, DEMOCRACY,

AND THE MEDIA

Laura Stein

UNIVERSITY OF ILLINOIS PRESS

URBANA AND CHICAGO

First Illinois paperback, 2008
Manufactured in the United States of America

1 2 3 4 5 C P 5 4 3 2 1

∞ This book is printed on acid-free paper.

The Library of Congress cataloged
the cloth edition as follows:

Stein, Laura Lynn, 1965–
Speech rights in America: the First Amendment, democracy,
and the media / Laura Stein.
p.   cm. — (The history of communication)
Includes bibliographical references and index.
ISBN-13: 978-0-252-03075-8 (cloth : alk. paper)
ISBN-10: 0-252-03075-3 (cloth : alk. paper)
1. Mass media—Political aspects—United States. 2. Freedom
of speech—United States. I. Title. II. Series.
P95.82.U6S737   2006
302.230973—dc22   2005031546

PAPERBACK ISBN 978-0-255-07536-0

CONTENTS

ACKNOWLEDGMENTS

THE SEEDS FOR THIS BOOK were planted at the former Annenberg Washington Program workshop in policy studies. A week of talks and presentations by Washington-based neoliberal and progressive communication-policy advocates impressed upon me the need to articulate a language and seek out a philosophy that effectively engages, and refutes, the reigning neoliberal policy approach. I hope I have found an alternative approach that will be useful to both scholars and activists committed to strengthening the democratic process.

The University of Texas at Austin has provided a supportive base from which to develop this project. A number of colleagues have read, commented upon, and ultimately improved this work at various stages. Thanks to John Downing for numerous and close readings of earlier drafts of this work. Thanks to David Braybrooke for helping to find terminology that describes the different approaches to speech rights within democratic liberalism. Thanks also to Sharon Strover and Tom Schatz for their helpful comments on this work. The many graduate students who have taken my course on communication, law, and power have helped me to continuously develop and refine my ideas. The Radio-Television-Film Department, with its critical, interdisciplinary, publicly minded, and active faculty and students, has provided a stimulating intellectual and social community, as well as many opportunities for the discussion of communication policy, democracy, and the public sphere. A sabbatical semester in the form of a UT Dean's Fellowship in the spring of 2005 helped me to complete this work in its final stages.

Thanks to a number of friends, colleagues, and media activists whose thoughts, insights, and interventions on media, politics, and policy over the years have been sustaining and inspiring. Special thanks to Dorothy Kidd, Dan Marcus, Cynthia Meyers, Tamara Ford, Laura Saponara, and folks at the Bay Area Alternative Media Network and the Paper Tiger Television Collective in New York.

Parts of this work have been presented at the International Communication Association, the International Association for Media and Communication Research, the University of California at San Diego, the University of Michigan at Ann Arbor, the University of Massachusetts at Amherst, and the University of San Francisco. Comments and questions posed in these forums spurred me to think about the work in new and different ways.

My thanks to Kerry Callahan, from University of Illinois Press, for adopting this project and to the anonymous reviewers whose comments called attention to the weak spots in the manuscript and offered very useful suggestions on how to strengthen them.

Finally, on a more personal note, thanks to my mother and father, who provided crucial support at the outset of this project. And my deepest thanks to my husband, Nikhil Sinha, who encouraged me to undertake this project, who diligently read numerous chapter drafts, and who supported me intellectually, professionally, emotionally, financially, and in just about every way imaginable.

Speech Rights in America

1 The First Amendment and Communication in Democratic Societies

THE FIRST AMENDMENT to the U.S. Constitution, which states that "Congress shall make no law . . . abridging the freedom of speech, or of the press," functions as the principle guarantor of speech rights in the United States. The First Amendment does not uphold all citizens' claims to free speech, however. In the latter half of the twentieth century, the First Amendment has not endorsed the right of responsible individuals and organizations to place paid advertisements on broadcast television. It has not protected the right of political candidates to print their replies in the pages of a newspaper that attacks them during an election. The U.S. Supreme Court decided in the 1970s that the public has no right to speak in print and broadcast media. Nor has the First Amendment supported a right to speak for community members who produce programming for public-access cable television or for Internet users who communicate over online service providers. The Supreme Court has not extended speech rights to citizens in either of these media. Programmers have no Court-confirmed speech rights on public-access cable channels, and Internet users have no right to send or receive electronic communications, including e-mail, over proprietary servers and other parts of the Internet's infrastructure. In these and other cases, opposing parties, namely those controlling information and communication technologies and those seeking access to them, have asked the courts to invoke very different interpretations of speech rights. By and large, the courts have favored interpretations that privilege the free-speech interests of media owners and operators over those of other speakers, whether these were political candidates and associations, public-access programmers, or Internet users.

This book is about competing interpretations of speech rights in the United States and why currently dominant First Amendment interpretations fail to protect a vision of speech rights appropriate to democratic societies. At its core, democracy is a system of governance in which politically equal citizens participate in their own self-rule. Democracy can also be said to require certain resources, capacities, and institutions that make self-governance possible. Some of these resources involve communication. Communication that serves democratic political processes, enabling citizens to deliberate over, define, and decide the common good, is the essence of democratic communication. The First Amendment fulfills its role as the guardian of speech rights in a democratic society when it protects the conditions necessary to democratic communication. First Amendment interpretations that fail to support these conditions or actively work against them alienate citizens from their rights and corrupt the essential workings of democracy.

At present, First Amendment interpretations only partially accomplish the task of safeguarding democratic speech rights, or speech rights necessary for democratic societies. While it is generally understood to protect the right to speak in public spaces and to prohibit government censorship, the First Amendment often abnegates speech-rights protections in the media. Rather than support speaking opportunities, public spaces, and access to information, the First Amendment is used as a tool for blocking avenues of public debate and discussion and striking down policy initiatives that create speaking opportunities for the broader public. For the most part, First Amendment interpretations applied to print, broadcast, and cable favor extensive speech rights for media owners and offer few and tenuous rights to the general populace.

If past First Amendment law is any indication of the future, the ability of the public to communicate over computer networks, like the Internet, may fare no better. Currently, people have many opportunities to engage in speech over computer networks, but no real rights. The legal regime, or system of rules, for the Internet has yet to take shape. Although today's Internet offers access under terms and conditions that favor democratic communication, changes in law, policy, and industry structure could effectively foreclose these opportunities. The future of democratic communication on the Internet may well depend on how First Amendment rights evolve over this medium.

The path to this future will be marked by discord. The First Amendment is a site where both competing definitions of speech rights and competing understandings of democracy itself do battle. This book locates the source of these clashes in liberal-democratic theory and considers the implications of divergent views of speech rights on communication law and policy and on the prospects for democratic communication in contemporary media. In the process, it contemplates the interrelationships among the political philosophical roots of First Amendment thought, contemporary legal constructions of speech rights, and the opportunities that people have to participate in democratic communication.

Speech Rights in Flux

The notion of an indeterminate and contestable First Amendment is unimaginable to many Americans. In the American popular consciousness, the First Amendment stands as an unassailable bulwark of individual freedom: unwavering, permanent, and solid. Yet, on closer inspection, the popular view falters. For the first hundred years of its existence, the First Amendment did little to protect speech rights. The amendment did not prevent some of America's founding fathers from enacting laws against speech that criticized government officials (the Sedition Act of 1798). Nor did it inhibit the city of Boston from denying a black minister the right to speak against racism in a public park (*Davis v. Massachusetts,* 1897). Indeed, history shows that for more than a hundred years after its enactment, the First Amendment failed to protect political dissent or the right to speak on public property. The belief that U.S. citizens have always had strong speech-rights protections is a modern myth.

Contemporary First Amendment law took shape primarily over two periods in recent U.S. history. First, in the decades between World War I and World War II free-speech law underwent a profound transformation. Events of the era, including the Great Depression, the New Deal, and the rise of the labor and progressive movements, precipitated a change in legal thinking on constitutional law (Kairys 257; Tribe 448–50). The Court became increasingly willing to uphold legislative interventions designed to alleviate the shortcomings of U.S. social, political, and economic life. The development of the rights to speak, to assemble, and to distribute literature on public property corresponded with the free-speech campaigns of labor and progressive activists who saw speech rights as an integral aspect of political organizing (Kairys 238, 246).[1] A Supreme Court decision to affirm the right to speak in public places stood at the pinnacle of this period of development. In *Hague v. CIO* in 1939, the Court endorsed the public's right to speak in public parks and delineated actual social spaces in which speech rights were protected, thereby creating for the first time in U.S. history practical opportunities for ordinary citizens to speak.

A second stage in the development of free-speech law occurred in the 1960s and 1970s. While the decades surrounding the 1930s saw an expansion of speech rights in unmediated public spaces, like streets and parks, this second era of First Amendment law dealt primarily with questions of media access (Ruggles 146). Since the 1960s, the Court has grappled with whether and to what extent the public has speech rights in the media. This issue has taken many forms. Does the public have a right of access to newspapers or broadcast channels? Do television viewers have a right to hear opposing viewpoints on controversial issues of public importance? Can the government restrict the dissemination of indecent content over broadcast stations and computer networks? Is the creation of public spaces for discussion on privately owned media a legitimate government undertaking? Should the government maintain a public sphere of information and knowledge through the creation of public spaces for democratic participation? In many cases, the judiciary has failed to provide decisive resolutions to these dilemmas. The answers to these questions have been, and continue to be, bitterly contested. Nevertheless, the First Amendment remains the most important tool that Americans have for dealing with questions of speech rights.

The configuration of speech rights in the media is particularly significant for democratic societies. In liberal democracies, rights protect the conditions necessary to democratic processes, demarcate opportunities for individual and collective action, and act as legal safeguards to democratic states (Bobbio). In today's communication environment, newspapers, radio, television, and computer networks have eclipsed public parks and street corners as relevant sites for political participation and discussion. These media are not only the dominant forums for communication, but they are inseparable from processes of political communication. Media influence people's perceptions of social reality and their evaluations of political events and phenomena (Gerbner; Graber; Iyengar and Kinder; Kraus and Davis). Media are also critical forums of public-opinion formation (Habermas; Garnham, *Capitalism and Communication*). The media have become an indispensable resource in modern democracies. As such, they must provide opportunities to engage in communication that supports and serves democratic processes and goals. The configuration of speech rights determines who can speak in the media and under what conditions, whether governments can maintain public spaces for democratic communication, and which cultural goods and resources will remain broadly accessible. How we understand and apply speech rights in the media has real effects on the practice of democracy. Speech rights can be interpreted in ways that alternately support or harm democratic communication.

In the opening decades of the twenty-first century, the meaning of speech rights in the media is again called into question. New technologies, particularly computer networks and related information services, threaten to undermine the speech regimes that presently govern media law. Under these regimes, speech rights apply differently, and often inconsistently, to different classes of media. In the print model, the speech rights of media owners are inviolate, and the public has no rights. The broadcast model allows the government to balance what are seen as the limited speech rights of the broader public against those of media owners. The common-carrier model, traditionally applied to the telephone, treats media owners as mere conduits of information with no associated speech rights. A hybrid model governs multichannel media, such as cable television, that retain printlike rights over the majority of their channels, but act as common carriers with respect to leased, public, educational, and governmental (PEG) access channels. Computer networks destabilize existing models by embodying media forms and services that cut across the traditional classifications. These networks, in which old media forms, including print, video, and voice-based communications, converge onto a new delivery platform, breed judicial uncertainty about which model of speech rights applies (Horwitz 23; Pool, *Technologies without Boundaries* 14). In addition, lawmakers and policy-makers increasingly assume that the relative abundance of media outlets will provide ample opportunities to exercise speech rights across the media sector as a whole. Judicial uncertainty, coupled with policy shifts that favor the liberalization and deregulation of communication industries, increasingly relegates determinations of speech rights to market mechanisms. But while markets are an efficient means of allocating communication resources, as I will argue shortly, they do not necessarily satisfy all of the conditions necessary for democratic communication.

Legal uncertainty, regulatory changes in media industries, inconsistencies in existing speech-rights regimes, and the rise of emerging and converging technologies suggest a need to reevaluate the relationship between the First Amendment, the media, and democratic communication. In this book, I reexamine these relationships and evaluate the extent to which First Amendment interpretations adequately protect democratic communication in today's media. In doing so, I assess current judicial interpretations of First

Amendment law and policy against a normative definition of speech rights in a democracy. In other words, I look at both how the law decides and how it *should* decide First Amendment cases. Developing a concrete, normative definition of democratic speech rights requires a return to first principles of liberal-democratic theory. Fundamental concepts, such as rights, liberty, democratic communication, and state action, form the basis of a normative definition of democratic speech rights. Grounded in democratic political theory, this definition can also provide needed policy principles for reevaluating and resolving contemporary speech-rights dilemmas.

Deciphering the First Amendment

Reinterpreting the First Amendment in accord with a more comprehensive vision of the role of communication in democratic society is not unfeasible. All First Amendment interpretations are grounded, explicitly or implicitly, in normative assumptions about political and social life. The rejection or acceptance of one legal theory over another ultimately turns on the selection of one theory of political or social organization over another. For example, before the 1930s, the courts adopted a laissez-faire approach to economic markets, striking down legislation like minimum-wage laws that interfered with the free market. After the Great Depression, judicial opinion about how markets should function changed. Courts began to view the marketplace as a social construct that could permit human intervention, rather than as the product of nature.[2] This change in thinking about economics made it possible for the courts to accept a host of New Deal reforms, including the creation of regulatory agencies like the Federal Communications Commission and the Federal Trade Commission (Sunstein 29–30). In a similar vein, different ideas about how to interpret speech rights revolve around which view of democratic theory a court adopts. The view that law is inextricably bound to political and social beliefs, held by both contemporary critical legal-studies scholars and the legal realists of the 1930s and 1940s who came before them, subjects the First Amendment to critical evaluation. It is the starting point for a critique of current legal doctrine and for the construction of alternative legal theories and rationales. The critical approach to law recognizes that legal decisions are affected by contemporary politics, economics, and culture, as well as by the ideologies and social structures that the law seeks to protect. Yet, this approach does not reduce the legal system to an ideological component of particular social structures. While the law exists to protect these structures, it is also an independent system that responds to an array of pressures and forces, including moral and ethical considerations (Rabinowitz 433). In this sense, law is both determined and has agency; it is a malleable instrument for defining the contours of social life. The direction of law can be altered if lawmakers apply alternative social or political theories to their understandings of the fundamental conflicts contained within particular legal domains.

A critical approach to law offers an alternative to popular First Amendment theories, like absolutism or historicism, that fall short of providing adequate interpretations of speech rights. The absolutist approach claims to offer a literal interpretation of the First Amendment. Absolutists argue that speech rights are safe as long as Congress and the states "make no law" affecting speech. For absolutists, aside from certain unprotected categories of speech such as obscenity or libel, absolutely no conditions exist that permit the government to regulate speech. While the simplicity of this theory is alluring, it is deceptive. It glosses over both the text and context of the First Amendment. Absolutism claims to derive meaning from the exact wording of the First Amendment, but it focuses on some words to the exclusion of others. The amendment does not state simply that "Congress shall make no law," but that "Congress shall make no law . . . *abridging*" speech rights. Since absolutists ignore the notion of abridgement, they do not differentiate between laws that expand or support and those that curtail speech. No speech laws are permissible. Furthermore, absolutism's tendency to be qualified in practice also mars its ostensible simplicity. Virtually no one advocates absolutism under all conditions. Even the staunchest absolutists favor government regulation of certain types of speech, such as obscenity, libel, blackmail, insider trading, or fraudulent commercial speech. In order to allow for these exceptions, absolutists classify some types of speech as conduct, resulting in a "qualified absolutism" (Smolla 24). These qualifications undermine absolutism's coherence and unity. Finally, this theory is indifferent to actual speaking opportunities in the media. Free speech exists wherever there is freedom from government intervention, but it does not require that anyone have a way, means, or outlet in which to speak. Absolutism presents a closed theoretical system that divorces itself from the need to assess the real-world conditions that enable or obstruct the exercise of speech rights.

Historicism likewise fails to provide a clear or comprehensive picture of the First Amendment. Historicism looks to the original intent of those who drafted the First Amendment to decipher its meaning. Yet, several factors prevent any uniform intent from manifesting itself. First, the First Amendment was drafted and adopted through a process that involved many people with diverse ideas and motivations. As with all legislation, the final product reflected a variety of influences and compromises put forth by multiple people with varying perspectives. Historical evidence shows that some framers believed that the First Amendment should prevent prior restraint of speech by the government, but not punishment of speech after the fact. Others believed that it should prevent both. In addition, some of the framers opposed including a bill of rights in the Constitution, but agreed to it ultimately because they recognized that some states would not ratify the Constitution without it. It is unclear that these framers had well-developed ideas about what the First Amendment should mean (Smolla 33, 37). For all of these reasons, extracting a single composite meaning from the mixed motivations and interests that went into establishing the First Amendment is untenable. Second, historical documents indicate that many of the framers' ideas about speech were in transition at the time that the First Amendment was drafted, as was thinking about free speech more generally. In the late eighteenth century, free speech could mean anything from prohibitions on censoring speech before it was disseminated to the right to speak out with impunity against the existing social order. While the former was endorsed in British common law, the latter was not. Some framers saw the First Amendment as a continuation of the conservative approach to speech rights set out in British common law, but others saw it as a uniquely American break with British tradition (Smolla 32). The First Amendment was drafted in a period of intellectual ferment during which individual and social views of speech rights were evolving. Third, some of the framers lent their rhetorical support to free speech, but acted in contradictory ways that complicate evaluations of the meaning behind their rhetoric. Most notably, none of the framers opposed laws against "seditious" speech, or speech that threatened to undermine the authority of the government. Given their concurrent support for the First Amendment, their failure to oppose sedition laws is an incongruity to modern sensibilities (Kairys 242). Finally, even were it possible to discern precisely what those who drafted the First Amendment meant by free speech, it would not automatically follow that contemporary understandings of free speech should be limited to definitions that were conceived in a radically different social and communicative context. Like the Constitution of which it is part, the First Amendment does not have a hard and fast meaning. Rather, as Laurence Tribe states, the Constitution is a deliberately indeterminate document designed to accommodate evolving political ideals and practices (iii).

As Tribe's statement suggests, the meaning of speech rights ultimately derives from the political system of which it is a part. Speech-rights interpretations draw on, and subsequently reinforce, basic assumptions of political philosophy. In liberal-democratic societies, ideas about the appropriate means and ends of democratic political life set the parameters for understanding speech rights. Definitions of speech rights may change over time, but they retain their foundation in liberal-democratic thought.

Speech Rights and Liberal-Democratic Traditions

Different views of speech rights have their origins in conflicting traditions within liberal-democratic thought. Broadly speaking, liberal democracies are those in which, in addition to all citizens participating in the process of self-governance, individual rights are a primary means of protecting liberty. While liberal-democratic theory generally recognizes that communication plays a key role in democratic political processes and that speech rights are a necessary means of protecting that role, divergent theoretical strands within the liberal tradition polarize over how best to achieve democratic speech rights. These different traditions within liberalism form the underlying conceptual framework for different views of speech rights. One strand of liberal theory, which stretches from eighteenth-century classical liberalism through contemporary neoliberalism, entrains what I call a defensive approach to speech rights. The defensive approach both stems from and shares the defining beliefs of classical and especially neoliberal theory—minimal state intervention and maximal scope for the free-market allocation of resources. From classical philosophers like Locke and Mill to more contemporary thinkers like Friedman, Hayek, and Nozick, the defensive approach defines liberty as the absence of coercion, particularly coercion by the state. In this approach, restraints on state action and the protection of private spheres of activity are considered sufficient guarantors of speech rights. An opposing strand of liberal-democratic thought, participatory-democratic theory, favors what I term an empowering approach to speech rights. Participatory-democratic theorists generally argue for greater citizen participation in democratic processes, the extension of democratic decision-making to key social institutions, and an adequate resource base for all citizens who would participate (Held, *Models of Democracy* 262). While some participatory democrats advocate the total democratization of all aspects of life, others like Barber more conservatively call for at least some participation some of the time in key areas of democratic life. The empowering approach to speech rights draws on this latter participatory-democratic tradition. Found in the work of Green, Dewey, Barber, and others, the empowering approach defines liberty or freedom in terms of people's abilities to act on their will or capacities and permits the state to create and protect the conditions necessary to ensure that freedom of speech is widely available. Elements of both theories of speech rights have been prevalent in policy debates and legal reasoning, though sometimes in diffuse and fragmented forms, throughout the history of media law and regulation. Foregrounding the role that these perspectives play in First Amendment case law provides insight into how liberal-democratic theory conditions thinking about speech rights.

The same terms and tenets that drive liberal-democratic theory also drive interpretations of speech rights. Ideas about the nature of rights, the relationship of individuals to society, the meaning of freedom or liberty, the proper domain of state action, and the conditions necessary to support democratic processes are part of an integrated system of political thought that lawmakers and policy-makers invariably draw on to settle legal conflicts over speech rights. In other words, definitions of speech rights and liberal-democratic theory share the same overarching philosophical framework, and it is this framework that explains both how First Amendment cases are decided and the contradictory nature of some of these decisions. Inconsistencies in First Amendment regimes, such as those that exist between broadcast and print media, and historical shifts in First Amendment interpretations reflect deeper schisms within liberalism over the interrelated concepts and ideas that make up this framework.

Unlike First Amendment theories that derive meaning from a particular value, set of values, or metaphor, an approach to understanding speech rights based in liberal-democratic theory is deeply and intimately connected to the existing framework for legal analysis. For example, values and metaphors may serve as organizing principles for understanding First Amendment aims and goals, like Baker's (*Human Liberty*) appeal to the values of individual self-fulfillment and political participation or Shiffrin's romantic image of the lonely dissenter, but their link to concrete legal traditions and arrangements is not always readily apparent. Reinterpreting law or countering legal precedent without this link is a formidable task. Other scholars concerned with the relationship between speech rights and democratic processes, like Meiklejohn, Emerson, and Sunstein, locate First Amendment meaning in the functions that speech should perform for democratic societies. For Meiklejohn (*Free Speech*), the meaning of the First Amendment derives from the necessity of self-government, which requires that all political speech relevant to democratic discussion and debate be heard.[3] Taking a somewhat broader view, Emerson includes individual self-fulfillment, the discovery of truth, participation in democratic decision-making, and the maintenance of stable, nonviolent communities among these functions (*System of Freedom* 6–8; "Legal Foundations" 2). Sunstein draws on the political thought of James Madison to identify the appropriate functions of democratic communication, which include exposing people to diversity, bringing attention to public issues and affairs, and enabling self-governance. While these theorists assert that government action is needed to ensure that the media can perform these functions, they gloss over the other elements of liberal-democratic theory on which First Amendment interpretations turn. As a result, these theories do not go as far as they could to counter the objections of liberal democrats who agree with them about the principal functions of democratic communication, but who disagree on the methods to achieve these goals and the meaning and definition of the central terms of liberal-democratic discourse.

Other scholars recognize the tendency of First Amendment law to clash over key concepts within liberal-democratic theory, but they focus on only one aspect of what is actually a wider set of interrelated differences. For example, Horwitz characterizes dominant traditions of First Amendment law as dividing over normative views of state action (22). Horwitz argues that "literal" interpretations of the First Amendment favor an absolute ban on all state action regulating expression, while "narrowly interventionist" interpretations demand that the state intervene in the media in order to protect the structures or conditions that enable free speech. Others, like Fiss and Parsons, argue that First Amendment theories divide over whether to favor the individual or the collective in resolving social conflicts. In their view, First Amendment frameworks pit the interests of the individual in being an autonomous agent in an unregulated society against the interests of the social collectivity in using affirmative government action to promote the free flow of information and vigorous public debate. These insights offer valuable, though only partial, explanations for radical differences in First Amendment theory. The fuller account I offer here, which examines the First Amendment in relation to a broader body of democratic theory, shows that First Amendment theory routinely invokes a range of interrelated democratic concepts. These concepts include not only state action and the individual-collective dichotomy, but also related ideas about the nature of freedom, the legitimate construction of rights, and the utility of assessing the actual conditions present in the communications environment.

Arriving at the best understanding of speech rights requires a critical evaluation of conflicting traditions within liberal-democratic theory. First Amendment meaning must be found in the most satisfactory account of democratic societies and democratic life. Contesting neoliberal theory from within the framework of liberalism, participatory theory challenges neoliberal discourse and definitions and provides a firm philosophical basis from which to rethink the meaning of speech rights. Although it has played a subordinate role in the development of media law and policy thus far, an empowering approach to speech rights offers the best means of safeguarding democratic communication in the twenty-first century.

Looking Forward, Looking Back

This book considers where First Amendment media law has been, where it is going, and where it should be going if speech rights are to become a usable resource for the majority of citizens. A close look at constitutional law reveals the status of speech rights in the media. Constitutional law, as decided by the Supreme Court, determines the scope of the First Amendment and the parameters of democratic communication in the United States. The Court analyzes, frames, and decides social conflicts over speech rights, often drawing on elements of political philosophy to help establish its interpretive and discursive framework. The philosophies that the Court chooses to follow have a profound effect on laws and policies, whose viability depends on whether they conform to current understandings of the First Amendment. Policies that ensure access to communication technology and services, protect people's ability to originate and send messages, promote diversity of media content, prevent exclusive control of information and cultural products, and create public spaces in otherwise proprietary media can be brought under the protective shield of a First Amendment that recognizes their value or decimated by a First Amendment impervious to their fate.

Current media law serves as both a link to the past and a signpost to the future. Every legal decision looks for precedents in the past tradition of legal thought. While law evolves over time, precedent ensures that threads of continuity always remain. Consequently, although the full picture of speech rights on computer networks is at present only partially sketched, we can expect past media law to provide the philosophical and theoretical templates for the mapping of First Amendment law onto this new territory. As with older media, the laws applied to new media during their formative period will be instrumental in shaping their development, structure, and use. Law and policy regimes applied to older media can act as maps that chart future policy paths.

Since the 1970s, communication law and policy have been shifting steadily toward neoliberal understandings of speech rights. The most obvious sign of this shift is the move away from viewing media owners as trustees of the public interest and toward a view that favors market forces as the best means to achieve communication-policy goals. The market model of regulation, also termed deregulation, prescribes that as new technologies emerge and old ones converge, the state should adopt a policy of noninterference with respect to all media.[4] The deregulatory perspective is evident in the 1996 Telecommunications Act, which liberalizes entry into broadcast, cable, and telecommunications markets, eliminates regulatory barriers that prevent media from competing in each other's markets, and relaxes market concentration and merger rules originally designed to limit the size and reach of media owners. The Court's current understanding of speech rights largely adopts and reinforces the assumption that competitive and deregulated media, operating in what is seen as the private sphere of the marketplace, necessarily satisfy the requirements of democratic communication.

Given the importance of media to democratic societies, this assumption must not go unquestioned. At the dawn of the twenty-first century, we approach a watershed in the development of communication technologies and policy. Older technologies like print, radio, and television are the dominant forums for popular communication. Speech-rights regimes applied to these media determine on a fundamental level how well they can function as agents of democratic communication among a citizenry. New technologies have the potential to create new opportunities for communication on a global scale. Yet, whether these new media will offer liberation or oppression, empowerment or exploitation, and relatively open communication or increased proprietary control over the communication environment hangs on whether they uphold the conditions and criteria necessary to democratic communication. If we want to steer policy toward the protection of the communication processes necessary to democracy, we must examine the course we are on and whether we are heading in the right direction. Liberal-democratic theory is the backdrop against which we must address these questions.

2   Rethinking Speech Rights

EVERY INTERPRETATION OF speech rights relies on ideas about democratic communication to give it meaning. But understandings of democratic communication are characterized by different, sometimes irreconcilable, visions of the role of communication in political and social life. Further clarifying what is meant by democratic communication and its link to speech rights is an essential step in any effort to interpret speech rights in a manner appropriate to democratic societies. The deep links between liberal-democratic theory and speech-rights interpretations are seldom thoroughly elucidated, however. Scholars who do address the relationship between speech rights and democratic communication turn most often to marketplace analogies, participatory-media theory, or social-rights approaches to explain the normative role of communication in a democracy and justify a preferred definition of speech rights to support that role. While these theories offer some useful and important insights, they fall short of providing adequate law and policy tools for regulating media and protecting speech rights in liberal-democratic societies. Before embarking on a closer analysis of liberal-democratic theory, I offer here a brief review of those theories most commonly used to advocate for preferred understandings of democratic communication and speech rights. I do so to underscore their theoretical contributions to understanding the requirements of democratic communication and their shortcomings when it comes to building the conceptual bridge needed to move from the realm of theory to adequate definitions of speech rights. As I will argue throughout this chapter, only liberal-democratic theory can provide that bridge.

Popular Theories of Democratic Communication and Speech Rights

Marketplace analogies have their roots in laissez-faire economic theory and draw on contemporary thinking about free markets, as well as the popular marketplace-of-ideas metaphor, to articulate their view of democratic communication. Justice Holmes's dissent in *Abrams v. US* (1919) offers the classic formulation of the marketplace-of-ideas metaphor. The metaphor holds that a free and competing trade in ideas is the best means of arriving at truth and knowledge. As Holmes stated in *Abrams,* "The best test of truth is the power of the thought to get itself accepted in the competition of the market" (630). Holmes did not believe that the best ideas would inevitably triumph in the market, but that vigorous debate free from government interference offered the best means of arriving at whatever comes to be accepted as truth (*Gitlow v. New York* 673; Ingber 3; Smolla 7–8). If the marketplace of ideas does not always produce truth, it at least tends to favor better ideas and to advance the greatest social good. Somewhat different from Holmes's more nuanced view, in contemporary usage the metaphor often invokes a romantic vision of a vibrant village market where the bustling economic exchange of information products results in well-informed citizens who have inspected, compared, and chosen the best goods available.

The marketplace-of-ideas metaphor also serves to bolster the application of economic free-market theory to ideas about democratic communication and speech rights. For those who advocate this marketplace approach, democratic communication is the inevitable outcome of well-functioning markets. In a competitive market, communication resources are abundant, and markets allocate these resources optimally to those who are willing and able to pay for them. Under this approach, ownership is the best arbiter of speech rights, and democratic communication is operative as long as people have exclusive control over the communication resources they own (Fowler and Brenner 237; Pool, *Technologies of Freedom* 133). In other words, speech rights will accrue to those with the resources and means to exercise them. In addition, marketplace advocates view government regulation of communication as antidemocratic. Regulation corrupts the free market for ideas by facilitating the inefficient allocation of resources, the threat of government censorship, and the violation of property rights. This neoclassical economic reading of the metaphor has increasingly dominated policy discourse (Napoli, "Marketplace of Ideas" 166).

The marketplace approach values the efficient and widespread circulation of communication resources and throws a spotlight on the potential dangers of government regulation of speech. But its vision of democratic communication is incomplete. The approach is hypersensitive to the power of government to disrupt communication in private spaces, but virtually oblivious to the ways in which economic power, operating through markets, can corrupt democratic processes. Market power can be as damaging and coercive as government power (Baker, "Giving the Audience"; Barron, "Access to the Press"). Later in this chapter, I will examine this assertion further. For now, I want to stress only that the marketplace approach has a limited analysis of power. It views government as the sole source of coercion and imagines the marketplace as a realm without coercive power relations. From this perspective, the marketplace is almost always a better means of allocating resources than its alternatives, no matter what conditions prevail in actual markets. The marketplace can be said to function well as long as a minimum competitive threshold is met. An oligopoly of media companies vying for consumer dollars, for instance, adequately meets this threshold. Under these circumstances, whether the market provides resources and opportunities for a broad array of people to communicate their perspectives is of little concern. Consumers' willingness to spend money on media products and services serves as their tacit approval of this arrangement. Furthermore, marketplace advocates are satisfied with conceptualizations of media market diversity that focus on the number of channels, outlets, and program formats, regardless of the diversity of viewpoints and sources present in the market. They do not consider whether ownership by a few major media companies or unfavorable access conditions for nonowners unduly restricts the range of viewpoints expressed. Nor do they examine whether or how different market practices affect opportunities for the majority of people to access and utilize the media (Barron, "Access to the Press"; Hopkins 44). In fact, the marketplace approach often defines democratic communication tautologically. Democratic communication is whatever the marketplace produces. Consequently, the market model has no strong, affirmative vision of the role of communication in democratic life. Aside from the presumption that ideas are best left to the marketplace, there is no conception of how communication can or should serve traditional democratic goals like representation, public-opinion formation, or agenda-setting. This approach offers an incomplete vision of democratic communication that is subordinate and secondary to market processes.

Another way that scholars understand democratic communication is through various participatory-democratic traditions. Scholarship in this vein, which I will refer to as participatory-media theory, might draw on sundry ideas such as Greek notions of direct democracy or the developmental democracy of J. S. Mill, who viewed political participation as essential to individual development. Alternately, it might reference the more radical developmental democracy of Rousseau, who believed that self-governance could not be alienated through representation, or the communitarian democracy of Arendt, Barber, and others, who emphasized public participation in communal life. Borrowing and combining elements of these and other participatory-democratic theories, many scholars assert a strong connection between democratic participation and communication and identify what they see as basic criteria for democratic communication. Taken as a whole, scholarship in the participatory tradition consistently argues that media in a democracy must include civic education, interest representation, and bona fide public spaces for discussion and debate. Because of their diverse orientations toward participatory-democratic theory, however, scholars who advocate this approach often disagree on precisely what these criteria mean or the extent to which they must be present in the media. For example, the media's role in fostering civic education can mean different things to different scholars. For Entman in *Democracy without Citizens,* civic education requires a press that cultivates citizen interest in politics, contributes to knowledgeable voting, and provides the tools for enforcing government accountability. Others, including Abramson, Arterton, and Orren, Enzensberger, and Rucinski, argue that civic education requires that media enable people to convey their experiences, mobilize their interests, and create the shared social knowledge necessary to legitimate democratic decision-making. In their view, civic education is not something that the press imparts to people, but something that people generate through active and direct participation in the formulation of public agendas and debates. Broad differences of opinion also crop up around the notion of representation. The participatory tradition posits that media must be able to represent all interests in society, regardless of the social or economic status of their proponents. Yet, the prescribed level of representation varies. Some maintain that inclusive representation requires that all citizens be able to convey their ideas and experiences to the larger community, as well as the total democratization of the media. Hagen, Kellner, and Splichal argue that representation necessitates direct control over the production, reception, and exchange of media content at all levels. Others argue that media with even a partial ability to serve democracy achieve adequate levels of representation. For theorists like Curran ("Rethinking the Media") and Tehranian, media that incorporate both public and market mechanisms can suitably promote the accessible and equitable organization of communication resources. Participatory-media theorists also advocate the need for public spaces in which to actualize democratic communication. Numerous theorists, including Curran ("Rethinking the Media"), Garnham (*Capitalism and Communication*), and Jakubowicz, maintain that the media must incorporate spaces that are universally inclusive, widely accessible, and insulated from the coercive power of both states and markets. This criterion is drawn from the public-sphere theory of Habermas, who sees the ideal public sphere as a site of rational and critical debate in which individuals achieve consensus on social questions and engage in legitimate public-opinion formation. While both government and economic power can undermine these spaces, governments bear the responsibility of maintaining and protecting these forums. Among participatory-media theorists, the concept of the public sphere variously justifies government support of public-service broadcasting; public access to media resources, institutions, and technologies; community media; and public or quasipublic spaces on privately held media.

Participatory-media theory insists on the centrality of communication institutions and processes to democratic societies. In this view, democratic communication does not involve the exchange of predetermined ideas in the marketplace, but the active and reflexive construction of ideas, opinions, and estimations of the common good. While this approach identifies some key criteria of media in a democracy, namely civic education, representation, and public spaces, its loose and often amorphous connection to the theoretical foundations of participatory-democratic theory limits its current strength and cohesiveness.[1] Theoretical eclecticism and inadequate attention to the fundamental terms and tenets of liberal-democratic theory curtail some of the potential usefulness of this work and make it difficult to apply to concrete institutions and practices. For example, actual public spaces require a legal and institutional basis in contemporary societies. It is not enough to say we must have public spaces. Scholars and analysts must show how these spaces fit within the bounds of current law and policy frameworks, including ideas of freedom, state action, and rights. Participatory-media theorists have yet to fully explore the fundamental connections between democratic communication theory and speech rights.

A third perspective on democratic communication holds that citizens of civilized societies are entitled to a basic level of communication resources, skills, and opportunities. These entitlements demarcate a set of communication rights that allow people to become full members of society. Building on the work of T. H. Marshall, theorists such as Murdock and Golding and Calabrese and Borchert argue that communication rights are part of the social rights of citizenship. According to Marshall, social rights "range from the right to a modicum of economic welfare and security to the right to share in the full social heritage and to live the life of a civilized being according to the standards prevailing in society" (8). Social rights guarantee that people have the resources and skill to exercise their civil and political rights, including the right to free speech. In fact, speech rights become substantive only when people have basic levels of education, information access, and other essential resources that make it possible for them to speak (Marshall 21; Murdock and Golding 183). Another version of this approach draws on the work of Sen, who argues that effective social entitlements must compensate for the fact that people are differently advantaged when it comes to achieving what they value. Applying Sen's ideas to communications, Garnham ("Amartya Sen's" 122–23) asserts that communication resources should enable people, despite their differential abilities, to pursue a range of social objectives, including improved job opportunities, better health care, and increased political participation.

The social-rights approach focuses on the level of entitlements that a just society must provide to impart a sense of belonging to its citizens and to assure them full participation in every aspect of social life. This approach rightly suggests that speech rights alone cannot satisfy the communicative needs of citizens. Rather, speech rights are a vital but insufficient condition for citizenship, which requires a broader array of communication opportunities and resources if these rights are to be meaningful. Yet, the strength of this approach is also its weakness. The social-rights approach posits a realm of communication rights and entitlements that stand apart from speech rights. Relying on communication rights to give content to the idea of democratic communication sidesteps questions about how to interpret speech rights and the relationship between speech rights and broader communication rights. These questions remain critical in countries where understandings of speech rights circumscribe the possibilities and limits for democratic communication through the media. In the United States, for instance, the communication rights advocated by this theory will stand or fall on whether they accord with current understandings of speech rights.

While marketplace theory lacks a normative vision of democratic communication, participatory and social-rights approaches suggest a range of principles and criteria that bring us closer to a fuller understanding of democratic communication. Of these latter approaches, participatory-media theory holds the most promise for understanding democratic communication, particularly when it draws from the liberal-democratic tradition. Yet, both participatory-media theory and social-rights approaches undertheorize the relationship between speech rights and democratic processes. The tendency to ground definitions of democratic communication within the framework of increased participation, the public sphere, or social rights often avoids direct confrontation with difficult questions posed by the dominant neoliberal interpretation of speech rights, interpretations that accord closely with the marketplace approach. These questions include the proper scope of state action, the meaning of liberty, and the conditions affecting democratic communication. Furthermore, interest in these questions has begun to transcend the American context as neoliberal paradigms assert themselves in other parts of the world, such as Europe and China (Keane xii; Zhao 51). To better understand the meaning and requirements of democratic communication, we must turn to the foundations of liberal-democratic theory itself.

In what follows, I examine the philosophical roots of competing definitions of democratic communication within liberal-democratic theory. In so doing, I aim to deconstruct and reconstruct the central terms of liberalism, to uncover the origins of conflicting views of speech rights, and to illuminate the relationship between speech rights and democratic processes in liberal-democratic thought. Comparing the main tenets of neoliberal and participatory-democratic theory in the liberal tradition, I argue that the latter, with its empowering view of speech rights, offers the best means of protecting democratic communication. This is so in part because participatory-democratic theory calls for the examination of the real conditions that affect speech. While neoliberal theory trusts the marketplace to provide adequate speaking opportunities, participatory-democratic theory insists on examining existing social conditions, whether the product of government or market constraints, that influence the ability to speak. In this view, the examination of actual conditions is an inevitable aspect of applying democratic principles to real-world situations (Bobbio 18; Held, *Political Theory* 4). In the latter part of this chapter, I argue that there are many ways in which today's communication markets distort democratic communication and that such distortions are likely to continue despite the advent of new technologies like the Internet. Recognition of prevailing market conditions, coupled with participatory-democratic theory, confirms the need for an empowering view of speech rights.

Neoliberalism and Defensive Rights

Neoliberalism is part of a long and complex tradition within political philosophy. The philosophical assumptions that animate neoliberalism wend their way from the classical liberalism of John Locke and J. S. Mill through influential modern thinkers like Friedrich Hayek, Milton Friedman, and Robert Nozick. These assumptions revolve around central terms and categories of liberal-democratic thought, including the nature of rights, the meaning of liberty, the proper domain of state action, and the relevance of real conditions to the exercise of freedom. Together, they form the philosophical core of a neoliberal approach to speech rights. This approach holds that free speech exists in private spheres, particularly the private sphere of the free market, shielded from government coercion. These assumptions likewise provide a series of focal points for charting the relationship between neoliberalism and defensive speech rights.

Like classical liberalism before it, neoliberalism focuses on the legal limits of state power. Neoliberals share the classical liberal belief that private individuals pursuing their goals with minimal state intervention is the best way to achieve the common good. Classical liberalism originated in the seventeenth century as an attempt to free civil society from tyrannical or absolutist political systems. As Held notes, classical liberals sought to liberate people from monarchical power by defining a private sphere free from state action (*Models of Democracy* 41). Closely linked to the mechanism of free markets and private property, this private sphere constituted the realm in which to exercise individual liberty. Neoliberalism, following this tradition, continues to advocate strict limits on state action as a guarantor of liberty, despite the fact that liberal states are no longer controlled by monarchs but by democratic publics.

Bound up with this notion of a private realm of freedom are correlative ideas about the nature of rights. Neoliberals follow Locke, the founder of philosophical liberalism, in presuming that individuals possess inherent rights that the government must protect. Locke believed that prior to society, people lived in a state of nature that corresponded to a "state of perfect freedom" in which everyone has a natural right to property, defined broadly as "their lives, liberties and estates" (243, 262). Although people possess freedom and rights in the state of nature, force or aggression on the part of others leads them to seek protection in society. By asserting that rights exist in a state of nature, prior to social formation, Locke sought to defend certain areas of life from government encroachment. For Locke, individuals do not derive rights to property or liberty from society. Rather, they maintain these rights against society. People consent to government authority only in order to protect property and liberty, and it is these rights that define the appropriate limits of government action. Locke's views resonate in the work of Nozick (14–19), who argues that people enter into society only in order to defend their rights and obtain justice, and in the writings of Friedman and Hayek, who assert the primacy of preexisting rights and the subservient role that government plays as the protector of these rights. For both classical liberals and neoliberals, liberty exists in that private realm of life where government cannot enter, and the role of government in protecting rights is primarily one of noninterference. These views set the foundation for a defensive approach to rights, which assumes that as long as a common authority exists to administer justice and protection, people are best able to exercise their rights when left to themselves.

Neoliberalism also invokes a particular definition of liberty that fuels a defensive view of rights. Liberty is the absence of coercion by the government and by others (Friedman; Hayek, *Road to Serfdom, Constitution of Liberty;* Nozick). Coercion refers to the ability of others to control our environment and to force us to act against our will (Hayek, *Constitution of Liberty* 21; Nozick 6). Neoliberalism draws a distinction, however, between individuals' ability to coerce one another and the impersonal contingencies of economic circumstance. When government or specific individuals directly limit our choices, coercion occurs. Coercion does not occur, however, when natural and inevitable market conditions limit our choices. Nozick pushes this view to its ultimate conclusion when he argues that, if market conditions put forward the choice of work or starvation, an individual's decision to work is not a matter of coercion, but a voluntary act of will (Nozick 262–64). Whether the marketplace provides real opportunities to exercise liberties like free speech is inconsequential to this view, which assumes that governments alone, and never competitive markets, have the power to coerce.

In addition to reasserting classical liberal tenets about the meaning of rights and liberties, neoliberalism contributes its own analyses of the relationship between markets and freedom to the liberal tradition. Neoliberals foreground the role of markets in democratic processes, arguing that liberty is both the precondition and outcome of competitive markets. Liberty is a precondition because economic progress relies on the ability of all individuals to act on their knowledge and experience in response to complex and dynamic social conditions (Friedman 4; Hayek, *Road to Serfdom, Constitution of Liberty*).[2] Freedom of action in the marketplace permits the unplanned coordination of economic activity that works to the mutual benefit of all members of society. Markets are coercion free, allowing free agents to enter into market transactions at their own discretion and only when it benefits them to do so. For Nozick, the free exchange of resources in the market constitutes the only just means of acquiring resources; any other method violates individual rights (149–50). Liberty is likewise the outcome of competitive markets. The market is a neutral realm that disperses and decentralizes power among a broad range of individual decision-makers (Friedman 12–13). Government coordination is inferior to market coordination. Political decision-making through governments inevitably fails because individuals cannot adequately comprehend or plan societies (Hayek, *Road to Serfdom* 50), because political power concentrated in government threatens liberty (Friedman 15), and because the state cannot legitimately interfere with individual actions and choices (Nozick 262–64).

The primary role of the state, according to neoliberalism, is to maintain the private sphere of individual liberty so closely identified with competitive markets. The state creates a framework for individually directed activity by maintaining monetary systems; protecting individuals against fraud, deception, and theft; enforcing contracts; preserving law and order; and generally ensuring the conditions necessary to a competitive market economy (Friedman 4; Hayek, *Road to Serfdom* 35). Friedman argues that the government should be viewed as an umpire who interprets and enforces the rules of the market. He says, "These then are the basic roles of government in a free society: to provide a means whereby we can modify the rules, to mediate differences among us on the meaning of the rules, and to enforce compliance with the rules on the part of those few who would otherwise not play the game" (25). Because the creation of a suitable economic framework is primarily a legal task, Held terms this model of politics "legal democracy" (*Models of Democracy* 251). Law sets the parameters for competition within the market, protects the institutions of competitive capitalism, and informs people of the predictable limits of government intervention.

Within the classical liberal and neoliberal tradition, notions of prior rights, liberty as the absence of coercion, strict limits on government action, and a symbiotic relationship between markets and freedom culminate in defensive speech rights. By and large, this approach pays scant attention to the role of speech in democratic processes, preferring instead to entrust free speech to competitive markets. In this view, speech rights exist in private spheres of activity in which the government cannot encroach. Even J. S. Mill, who perhaps more than any other liberal theorist acknowledged the normative dimensions of democratic communication, adhered to a basically defensive approach to speech rights. As a utilitarian liberal, Mill believed that rights delineate areas in which individuals are to be left alone and that strict limits on state action, as well as laissez-faire economic policies, offered adequate protection to rights and liberties.[3] Yet, Mill carved out a role for democratic communication atypical of the classical liberal tradition.[4] In *On Liberty*, Mill argued that free speech was necessary to the development of individuality, essential to democratic discussion and opinion formation, and central to the utilitarian project of associating self-interest with the long-term social good. In addition, Mill recognized that government was not the only threat to free speech. The tyranny of public opinion could also work to suppress the diverse viewpoints necessary to democratic communication (56). Despite this recognition, Mill operated within an essentially defensive framework. He argued that free speech could be protected by imposing strict limits on government action and by imploring the public to restrain from its urge to censor.

Neoliberals conceptualize free speech wholly in terms of the marketplace. For Hayek, democratic communication requires the existence of a sphere for opinion formation that is independent of government or majority control (*Constitution of Liberty* 109). Competitive markets, as private spheres free from government coercion, adequately satisfy this requirement. Further-more, aside from structuring markets to be competitive, the limited role of government under neoliberal theory allows the state virtually no scope to regulate communications markets. For Friedman, even federal regulation of radio and television oversteps the government's primary role of maintaining markets and thereby constitutes an implicit violation of speech rights (35).

Liberal Participatory-Democratic Theory and Empowering Speech Rights

Modern participatory-democratic theory in the liberal tradition presents a formidable critique of classical liberalism and neoliberalism, as well as an alternative way of viewing the question of speech rights.[5] Participatory-democratic theory takes apart and reconstructs neoliberal definitions of rights, liberty, state action, and the role of communication in democratic societies. One thread of this theory, which sheds light on the connections between speech rights and democratic processes, begins with T. H. Green's criticism of classical liberalism and culminates in the pragmatic and commu-nication-centered democratic theory of John Dewey and Benjamin Barber. Taken together, the work of Green, Dewey, and Barber supports an empow-ering view of speech rights. In this view, democratic communication resides in public spheres and spaces where people can speak free from all forms of coercion. Grounded in a philosophical understanding of the role of speech in democratic societies and open to an assessment of actual opportunities to speak in contemporary media, participatory-democratic theory lays the theoretical foundation for an interpretation of speech rights better suited to democracy.

Moral philosopher T. H. Green provides a starting point for the revision of both neoliberal theory and defensive speech rights. Writing in mid-nineteenth-century Britain, surrounded by what he saw as the deleterious effects of industrialization, Green rethought classical liberalism's central terms and purposes. Green argued that individuals do not participate in society and obey laws in order to satisfy their utilitarian desires, but rather to secure the conditions necessary for the exercise of free will. Like the classical liberals, Green held that freedom requires the absence of coercion or constraint. But, for Green, the absence of coercion is a necessary but not sufficient condition for freedom. Freedom necessitates both a coercion-free environment and the affirmative ability to act on one's will and capacities. Freedom is "a positive power or capacity of doing or enjoying something worth doing or enjoying, and that, too, something that we do or enjoy in common with others. We mean by it a power which each man exercises through the help or security given him by his fellow-men, and which he in turn helps to secure for them" ("Liberal Legislation" 21). For Green, freedom is a positive right that exists only in communities. The state, as a manifestation of community, enforces rights and obligations so individuals can exercise their capacities to pursue the common good and act as moral beings. Ultimately, only rights that contribute to the overall common good are capable of receiving community recognition.

Green observed that while the state is a potential source of coercion, coercion is not unique to the state. Economic and social conditions generated by private-sector practices can also constitute coercion. The state is morally obligated to protect people from these nongovernmental constraints, which include practices such as exploitative private contracts and bad working conditions. In addition, not every state action is coercive. In some cases, state action works to secure conditions conducive to freedom. For instance, laws designed to protect the weaker party in a contract or to ameliorate unhealthy or unsanitary working conditions promote, rather than quash, freedom. Green's concept of positive freedom, in which the state safeguards the power of the individual to pursue his or her idea of the common good, gave more latitude to state action than classical liberals would allow. At the same time, Green argued that the state should protect rights in an unobtrusive, or negative, way. The state must make it possible for individuals to realize their own will and the common good, but it should never compel them to do so (*Lectures* 45).

Participatory-democratic theorists, including American pragmatists Dewey and Barber, incorporate Green's ideas about freedom and state action and extend these to construct a vision of liberalism dedicated to participatory-democratic processes. Unlike classical liberals and neoliberals, pragmatists do not aim to defend established political truths through democracy, but to institute procedures for reaching social agreement on what is accepted as truth. Their democratic vision reflects the American pragmatist tradition, which stresses the importance of reasonable choice and action in the absence of knowable truths, particularly where politics is concerned. Pragmatism readjusts the focus of liberal politics from questions of ontological truth to the epistemological processes by which people determine concepts of truth and knowledge (West 213). As Rorty notes, instead of seeking essentialist notions of truth, pragmatists search for social agreement about what it is good to believe (162–63). For Dewey and Barber, democracy is not a defense against authoritarian power, but the best method for coming to know and understand the social world and for making collective decisions about social life.

Both Dewey and Barber take community or association as a simple fact of human existence. The association of individuals is a universal human characteristic that requires no political explanation. Consequently, Dewey and Barber reject the neoliberal contention that rights exist outside of social formations. For them, rights are the product, not the predecessor, of community. The invention of both law and politics, rights are community-sanctioned social constructs that give people protections they would not have outside society (Barber 89; Dewey 12). Consequently, rights are not held against society, but rather through it. Nor is the relationship between the individual and the state one of inherent antagonism. Rather, this relationship is symbiotic, cooperative, and interdependent. Dewey and Barber, along with other participatory-democratic theorists, argue that the public and the state mutually constitute one another. Self-governing citizens make use of the state as an agent for collective action, while the state creates and enforces the benefits of citizenship (Dewey 33; Barber 152). Though the state may potentially harm liberty, it is also the only means by which the public can ensure the protection of rights and freedoms.

Following Green, liberal participatory-democratic theory adopts a view of freedom that runs counter to that of classical liberalism and neoliberalism. Freedom denotes the positive capacity to enact one's will and is not tidily synonymous with the absence of government coercion. Freedom requires liberation from external constraints, whether they originate in the economy or the state, and the positive ability of individuals to choose between significant alternatives (Bobbio; Dewey; Held, *Political Theory;* MacCallum). People must be free from coercion and free to act in the social world. Consequently, protecting freedom requires safeguarding opportunities for action against all types of coercion.

Rather than emphasize the limits of government action, participatory democrats argue that the state must promote and protect rights, freedoms, and other conditions necessary to political participation. Barber looks to the state to institute strong democracies that give all citizens the opportunity at times to govern themselves in important public matters. As the instrument through which the public organizes itself, the state must cultivate processes, institutions, and forms of citizenship that promote reasonable community judgments and choices. Dewey argues that the state should not be alienated from the public or limited to acting as the umpire or referee of social interaction (73). Moreover, while the state's main duty is to serve the public, its precise functions may vary along with concomitant changes in the world. According to Dewey (74), "Just as publics and states vary with conditions of time and place, so do the concrete functions which should be carried on by states. There is no antecedent universal proposition that can be laid down because of which the functions of a state should be limited or expanded. Their scope is something to be critically and experimentally determined." Political structures, says Dewey, must be able to adapt and respond to changes across such vital areas of social life as the economy, technology, and communication. Observation of the real conditions of social life and experimental regulation in the public interest should determine the precise aims and functions of a state at any given moment. Unlike neoliberal theorists who define freedom without reference to real-world conditions, participatory democrats recognize that any definition of freedom must be informed by the historical and social contexts that shape its real life applications.

In addition to redefining fundamental liberal terms, participatory-democratic theory, particularly as expressed in Dewey and Barber, foregrounds the role of communication in democratic politics. Both Dewey and Barber argued that human association inevitably leads to conflicts and consequences that are in the public's interest to regulate or control. The need to act in a world where political and social knowledge is subjective and uncertain is the very genesis of politics. As Barber states, "The need for politics arises when some *action* of *public* consequence becomes *necessary* and when men must thus make a *public choice* that is *reasonable* in the face of *conflict* despite the *absence of an independent ground* of judgment" (122, emphasis original). For Barber, as for Dewey, politics is a response to the simple fact that there is no general agreement as to social and political truths and that democratic politics is the best way to reach agreement. For Dewey, who worried that modern publics no longer had the means to recognize, articulate, and respond to problems brought on by industrial organization, this meant encouraging democratic organization on a scale commensurate with the consequences of associated life (156). As pragmatists, both argued for the need to strengthen the processes by which communities collectively examine, debate, and decide how to achieve the common good. If democratic life consists of the public being able to recognize and act on its interests, communication is the method by which communities come to know themselves and the world around them. It is the tool that allows them to evaluate social experience, to make reasoned political judgments, to discern the public good, and to democratically structure the consequences of associated life. Communication generates the necessary social knowledge for effective self-government and legitimizes democratic action by securing the active consent of citizens who are able to identify their self-interests with a larger view of the common good.

Social mediation is the central function of communication in democratic societies. Communication acts as a social mediator when citizens share their unique opinions and perspectives and develop knowledge of their diverse social experiences (Dewey 155; Barber 137). In the pragmatist tradition, knowledge is a social phenomenon. People attain knowledge only by circulating the full range of social insights, opinions, and experiences. For Dewey, social inquiry and social knowledge require the freedom to speak and disseminate one's thoughts. He notes, "There can be no public without full publicity in respect to all consequences which concern it. Whatever obstructs and restricts publicity, limits and distorts public opinion and checks and distorts thinking on social affairs. Without freedom of expression, not even methods of social inquiry can be developed" (167). Freedom of speech is the fulcrum of democratic communication and, by extension, legitimate public opinion. Further, free speech is a positive freedom; it cannot be protected simply through exemption from legal restrictions. Free speech, like other positive freedoms, must offer real opportunities for public participation in democratic processes on a scale commensurate with the consequences of associated life (168).

Barber likewise argues that social mediation depends on real opportunities to communicate and that democratic "talk" is the key to legitimate political processes. Democratic talk performs a number of functions vital to democratic societies. These include *agenda-setting* as the grassroots formulation of issues and problems; *exploration of mutuality* in thoughts, feelings, and experiences; *affiliation and affection* through the development of feelings, concerns, and empathy for others; *maintenance of autonomy* by consistently reexamining one's convictions; *witness and self-expression* through the expression of convictions, dissent, frustration, and opposition; *reformulation and reconceptualization,* or the reshaping of political terms and values; and *community-building* through the creation of publicly minded citizens who recognize common interests and common goods (Barber 182–97). By defining democratic talk in the broadest possible terms, Barber avoids the pitfall of recognizing only the most overtly political speech as relevant to democratic communication. His broad taxonomy of democratic talk suggests an inclusive approach to the types of speech that need to be present in the media. For Barber, democracies must support local and national institutions and forums that enable communities to engage in a full range of democratic talk (273–79).

Viewed together, Green, Dewey, and Barber offer a critique of classical liberalism and neoliberalism capable of constructing a practical and concrete definition of democratic speech rights. While they do not always address the question of speech rights directly, their work suggests a view of speech rights that is closely tied to democratic processes and the fundamental tenets of liberalism. The work of these and other participatory-democratic theorists points to an empowering approach to speech rights. This approach recognizes the constructed nature of rights, defines freedom positively as the opportunity to act, and requires governments to ensure that opportunities to speak exist within a given set of social conditions. Though the state is a potential source of censorship, it is also the only means by which the public can regulate media to serve the interests of democratic societies. In the eyes of participatory democrats, neoliberal strictures against government action, blind reliance on market processes, and disregard for the impact of real-world conditions on individual freedom diminish democracy. Concentrating on the need to develop procedures, processes, and institutions that support the acquisition of social knowledge and legitimate public decision-making, participatory-democratic theory strongly suggests a set of communicative requirements for democratic societies. These requirements include the maintenance of media that enable social mediation, the availability of public spaces that are free from coercion of all kinds, and a democratic state that is authorized to secure these conditions. The central differences between defensive and empowering approaches to speech rights are summarized in table 1.

The idea of social mediation encompasses several issues germane to communication law and policy. Social mediation implies the circulation of information both to and from various members of the public. In simple legal parlance, we could say that social mediation requires the right to originate or send information and the right to receive information. The right to send information ensures that citizens are able to represent their diverse interests and concerns to the broader community. Social mediation also demands that the public be able to attain a broadly representative range of ideas and opinions. Thus, the right to receive communication completes the mediation process, guaranteeing that potential viewers, listeners, and readers can access a plurality of information and viewpoints. The view of democratic communication as social mediation contrasts sharply with neoliberal perspectives that assume that individuals create political knowledge when they transmit their autonomous, rational, and preformed ideas to one another (Peters). Participatory-democratic theory subscribes to what Carey terms a "ritual view" of communication, or one that identifies communication with processes of sharing and participation, and rejects a "transmission view" that defines communication as "imparting," "transmitting," or "giving information to others" (15, 18). By definition, social mediation does not originate in one source or set of sources to be imparted to the masses, but must encompass the mutual exchange of insights and opinions among the wider public.

TABLE 1

Defensive Speech Rights	Empowering Speech Rights
Freedom exists in private spheres and spaces.	Freedom exists in public spheres and spaces.
Government coercion threatens freedom.	Government and market coercion threaten freedom.
All state action constitutes coercion.	State action can protect speech opportunities.
Rights are guaranteed by restraints on state action.	Rights require the positive ability to act on one's will and capacities.
Real conditions of speech markets are irrelevant.	Real conditions of speech markets are relevant.

While neoliberals argue that freedom occurs in private spaces that are devoid of government coercion, participatory democrats maintain that the exercise of rights requires public spheres and spaces in which individuals have real opportunities to act on their will and capacities. Whether coercion originates in the economy or the state is inconsequential in this view. What matters is the public nature of democratic communicative space. Unlike classical liberal and neoliberal thinkers, however, participatory democrats do not draw a neat separation between public and private space based on government or market activity. For participatory theorists, social activities and actions take on a public dimension whenever they have significant consequences for the greater community (Dewey 15). Markets and governments do not provide an automatic or easy dividing line between what is private and what is public. Governments everywhere organize and enforce economic relations, rendering market structures no more natural, inevitable, or self-sustaining than political structures. At the same time, markets can act as public spaces if they provide the requisite opportunities to exercise rights. In addition, since public spaces will in any case exist in relation to markets or governments, they can never be entirely separate from either (Fraser). From the vantage point of participatory-democratic theory, we can follow Mosco in defining the "public" in public space as "a set of social processes" that promote democracy and democratic decision-making (170). This definition suggests that law and legislation can open up public spaces on both publicly and privately supported media. Participatory-democratic theory asserts that it is the government's responsibility to create these spaces if they do not otherwise exist. A prime mechanism for doing so is the legal creation of public spaces where citizen speech rights are primary. Critically, law must not foreclose the possibility of the government maintaining or bolstering the public sphere by devaluing or categorically dismissing the legitimacy and legality of government-created public spaces. Ultimately, public space is not defined by its ownership or financial means of support, but by its commitment to the implementation of democratic processes that offer real and widespread opportunities for participation in democratic communication. This does not mean that everyone must have complete and unfettered access to all media all the time. Such a plan would be neither efficient nor effective. It does mean that opportunities to speak and access information must be available when needed and that everyone has some opportunity to engage in democratic talk at least some of the time.

Finally, participatory-democratic theory suggests that democracies must pay attention to the real and dynamic conditions that enervate or invigorate freedom. When markets fail to provide conditions in which freedom becomes operative, participatory theory looks to the state to create and protect these. It is the duty of the democratic state to ensure that citizens can exercise their rights. Though the state secures them, these spaces are not subject to state control and censorship. The state must make it possible for individuals to exercise their speech rights without restriction or coercion by either public or private agents. To this end, the state can implement neutral laws and policies that entail equal treatment of all parties and that function in a predictable and consistent manner.

In practice, there is a longstanding tradition in the United States of government regulation where markets fail to achieve social goals. However, marketplace advocates who recognize only the most limited forms of market failure and reject empowering speech rights threaten this tradition. For many free marketers and neoclassical economists, market failure occurs only when markets do not produce efficient outcomes for technical reasons. Examples of technical market failure include the phenomenon of "missing markets" (where there is no market for clean air, for safety, or for a stable environment) and the failure of private industries to produce public goods (such as highways, national currency, and national defense). But despite their ability to function efficiently, markets may produce outcomes that are unacceptable to the public (Sheffrin). If well-functioning media markets fail to provide adequate opportunities for democratic communication, we might also legitimately see this as a type of market failure, although neoclassical economics is not willing to acknowledge it as such. In this case, markets would have failed because they did not meet legitimate societal needs and goals. Yet, in a legal environment that increasingly favors defensive speech rights, the ability of governments to respond to such market failure becomes progressively circumscribed.

Speech rights set the parameters in which communication can occur. As such, they must protect the communicative requirements of democratic societies. According to participatory-democratic theory, these requirements include the guarantee of public spaces dedicated to social mediation and insulated from oppressive real-world conditions. Participatory-democratic theory does not, however, undertake substantive analysis of the communicative conditions found in today's media. Nor should it. As a political philosophy, participatory-democratic theory is normative by nature. It studies what constitutes a good or ideal society (Strauss). It does not assess the structure and practices of contemporary markets. The structure of media resources, the terms of access to them, and the economic pressures shaping political and cultural expression are all factors that may affect the social mediation process. Only the examination of actual media systems can determine whether government intervention is necessary to protect speech rights or whether these rights may safely be left to market mechanisms.

When Markets and Democracies Clash

Democratic communication requires that citizens be able to speak through the media and access a range of communication that is broadly representative of social thought and experience. Social mediation of this type occurs when information and communication address and represent the diverse needs and values of all members of the public at least some of the time. An important question for democratic societies, then, is whether commercial media operating along market principles permit social mediation to flourish. Neoclassical economists argue that markets are the best way to organize media, resulting in the optimal socioeconomic good. However, a growing number of media researchers and economists argue that markets alone do not inevitably produce outcomes that support democratic goals. Rather, rational marketplace behavior can systematically deter media from discovering and serving the public's needs. A closer look at media markets and their shortcomings provides ample evidence that the public cannot rely on markets alone to protect democratic communication. An empowering view of speech rights is necessary to ensure that governments can create opportunities for democratic communication when even well-functioning markets fail to provide them.

Neoclassical Economics on Media Markets

Neoclassical economics holds that competitive markets, not public regulation by governments, are the best way to allocate a society's resources and satisfy individual wants and needs. In a competitive market, consumer demand determines what goods are produced and who obtains them. Consumers express their preferences for goods and services through their willingness to pay.[6] The more intensely they prefer a good, the more they will pay for it. Producers compete with each other to meet consumer demand, offering the goods that consumers desire at a price that allows the producers to profit. Markets are self-regulating. Market participants acting in their respective self-interests ensure that the market produces goods and services that people want at prices acceptable to both buyers and sellers. Competitive markets are also efficient. They ensure the optimal allocation of scarce resources by maximizing industry productivity, providing consumers with what they want in the amounts needed, and continually adjusting to fluctuations in consumer demand. While the market values efficiency first and foremost, an efficient economy can also be said to serve the public good by maximizing the wealth of the nation. In this view, the outcomes of efficient markets, whatever they may be, inevitably increase the social welfare. The government's only role in this model is to make and enforce the rules that allow competitive markets to function. Many economists, such as Posner, Stigler, and Hilton, view government-determined public service regulations as costly and politicized interventions that pervert the efficient operation of the marketplace.

In the United States, media have long been subject to regulation by both the marketplace and the government. Both create rules and restrictions that govern the operation of media industries. Commercial media operate according to market principles and axiomatically aim to maximize profit and the value of their firms (Albarran; Gomery; Picard, *Media Economics*). At the same time, the government has always placed some public-interest or public-service constraints on media designed to address the shortcomings of the marketplace. Since the late 1970s, however, marketplace advocates have sought to limit government's hand in social regulation and to bring the media wholly under the marketplace approach. Fowler and Brenner offered the rationale for a more market-oriented media in a classic 1982 law review article. Although they wrote about broadcasting in particular, their argument encapsulates the neoclassical perspective on all media. Fowler, then chairman of the FCC, and Brenner, his legal assistant, argued that broadcasters could best serve the public interest by responding to market forces rather than to extramarket regulation imposed by the government. For Fowler and Brenner, the market for information goods is a highly competitive one in which market mechanisms can best express and satisfy the public's wants and needs and, by extension, the public interest. While they acknowledge that the market for broadcasting is indirect, they assert that it nevertheless allows broadcasters to discover and respond to audience demand. In the broadcast market, advertisers—not audiences—provide financial support for broadcast programming. As a result, audiences cannot express the intensity of their preferences through their willingness to pay for programming. Yet, indirect market mechanisms work to express audience demand in any case. Because advertisers seek to attract the largest possible audience, they gravitate toward programming with the highest ratings. Broadcasters who want to maximize their profits address audience demand by providing programming designed to attract the large audiences that advertisers demand. In this way, the interests of advertisers and audiences align, and broadcasters respond to audience demand in the very process of serving advertisers. Government regulation that determines what the public needs disrupts the market's allocation of goods and results in programming decisions that ignore the well-functioning, if indirect, expression of consumer demand.

For neoclassical economists, commercial media markets work well whether audiences express their preferences directly or indirectly. Nonadvertising-supported media that rely on customer subscription, like some premium cable channels or satellite radio, or those that rely on direct sales, such as book publishers, allow consumers to express their preferences directly through their willingness to pay for these products. Media that are entirely advertising supported, such as broadcast television and radio, or partly advertising supported, such as newspapers, magazines, and most cable channels, allow media producers to gauge consumer demand through indirect mechanisms. In addition, there are important societal benefits associated with advertising-supported media. By providing all or part of the revenues of media firms, advertising support can subsidize production budgets and, consequently, reduce the cost at which firms offer their products to consumers. The end result is media that are more affordable for everybody. Advertising support also functions to efficiently bring the most desired programs to the greatest number of people. Since media advertising rates are based largely on the number of people reached, media firms have incentive to produce programs that attract the greatest numbers. Audience measurements like ratings express audience behavior and preferences and give audiences in aggregate the ability to influence media content and firms (Webster and Phelan 18–20). For market advocates, efficient media markets also translate into adequate performance in the metaphorical marketplace of ideas (Entman and Wildman). Audience demand expressed through market mechanisms ensures that people generally receive as much media diversity, variety, and quality as they desire and that only unpopular products or services for which there is relatively little demand fail to emerge or survive.

While neoclassical economics highlights the societal benefits and efficiencies of media markets, it does not offer a complete or accurate picture of media market behavior. Others have shown that media markets are deficient on several counts when it comes to giving people what they want or need, particularly in a democracy. Market processes fall short of indicating or satisfying consumer preferences in several ways. Advertising support results in a narrowed range of media content that serves advertiser interests above the interests of actual audience members. While consumer-supported media allow for the direct expression of consumer interests without the content distortions introduced by advertisers, this model fails to make media available to those who cannot afford it. For the majority of media that are publicly traded, the stock market intensifies the negative effects of market forces on media content. Publicly traded companies routinely place profits above the quality of their product and the interests of stockholders above those of consumers. These marketplace realities suggest that media markets are not an entirely sufficient means of producing and allocating communication resources in democratic societies, which require that media reflect the full range of interests of all sectors of society at least some of the time.

Advertising, Media Behavior, and Content Constraints

Many media serve advertisers first and audiences second. Media economists widely recognize that media often have two distinct, though interrelated, patrons and products. They sell content and services to consumers, and they sell audiences to advertisers (Napoli, *Audience Economics;* Picard, *Media Economics;* Smythe; Sparks 38–39). Advertising-supported media aim to attract audiences in order to package and sell them to advertisers. Advertisers buy the audience product in order to gain the time and attention of individuals who are likely to purchase their products. While nearly all media are actively engaged in both the content and audience-product markets, the latter probably has more influence on media content. This is because the audience product generally accounts for the greater part of many media firm revenues. Overall, advertising comprises 70 percent of newspaper revenues, 100 percent of broadcast radio and television revenues, and 60 percent of national cable-television revenues (Napoli, *Audience Economics* 18). The need to attract advertisers and the audiences they want to reach is a driving force behind many firms systematically shaping the parameters of media content and behavior. And while the interests of advertisers and audiences may at times converge, they are far from synonymous, as Fowler and Brenner insist. Ultimately, advertisers are interested in only some audience members, not the entire media audience. Advertiser-supported media are unlikely to produce content that holds little or no interest for advertisers or their preferred audiences, even if it holds great interest for other audience segments. Moreover, advertiser influence over content precedes audience influence (Turow, *Media*

Industries 21). Advertiser interests can determine the shape and character of available media products before these ever reach the public.

Audience size is of prime importance to advertisers who want their messages to reach large numbers.[7] The need to reach large numbers ensures that advertisers will support media that can attract large audiences. Advertisers and media firms use audience-measurement data to determine the exchange value of the audience product, and this value is partly a function of audience size. But the need to reach large numbers can have an inhibiting effect on media content. Media that are compelled to attract large audiences feel pressure to produce content that will predictably assemble these audiences. Gitlin's study of primetime television network programming practices found that the need to attract large audiences caused network executives to cater to established audience tastes, rely on the recycling of previously successful program ideas, and avoid innovative and challenging programming. Baker's study of the rise of advertising as a mode of support for newspapers strongly suggests that newspapers came to avoid partisan reporting and controversial content in order to increase their audience reach (*Advertising and a Democratic Press*). Likewise, Napoli attributes the media's lack of content diversity to the need to predictably garner large audiences for advertisers (*Audience Economics*). Advertisers' need for large audiences results in conservative programming and content strategies designed to reliably fetch mass audiences. This economic model does not cater to smaller audiences with marginal interests and tastes or to the more heterogeneous interests of large audiences, but to the lowest common denominator of mass audience interests.

In addition, advertisers are not interested in reaching all audience members, but in maximizing their preferred audience (Napoli, *Audience Economics;* Picard, *Economics and Financing;* Shoemaker and Reese 163). Audience-measurement systems are concerned not only with audience size, but also with the demographic characteristics of audiences, including most commonly their age, gender, income, language, and ethnicity. The preferred audience is one that advertisers perceive as being most likely to buy their products. Typically, the preferred audience is young, possesses a high income, and is not part of an ethnic minority. Although people over the age of 50 make up half of the actual primetime broadcast-television audience and a substantial percentage of the broadcast-television audience generally, television advertisers are primarily interested in reaching the 18–49 age group, who are perceived as less set in their buying habits and more likely to try new products (Gitlin 60; Ross; Turow, *Breaking Up America* 74–75). In addition, advertisers place less value on reaching minority audiences, which can result in less advertising revenues for media that target ethnic minorities (Bettig and Hall 5; Napoli, "Internet" 113–14). A study conducted by the Civil Rights Forum on Communications Policy found that minority radio broadcasters reported having to offer advertising time at severely discounted rates compared to their counterparts who catered to equally sized general audiences. Thus, if two radio stations have the same audience size, but one caters to African Americans or Latinos and one to a majority white audience, the latter will have higher ad revenues and more money to develop content aimed at its target audience. Researchers have found a similar phenomenon operating with respect to different classes of newspaper readers (Curran, "Impact of Advertising" 321; Hirsch and Gordon; and Sparks 39). In the case of two newspapers with the same cover price and same audience size, the paper with the typically preferred audience generated greater advertising revenues, higher profits, and more resources for editorial content than the paper serving the less valued audience. In such cases, differential valuation of audiences by advertisers transforms socioeconomic differences into unequal subsidization of cultural goods. Advertisers will pay more to reach audiences with the demographic characteristics they desire. Routinely excluded from consideration are those whom advertisers see as less likely to buy their products, including the old, the very young, the poor, and racial and ethnic minorities, even though many of these may consume media in greater numbers and more frequently than more valued demographic groups.

The media position themselves to offer specific audience segments to advertisers through content production. Many scholars have concluded that there are powerful incentives for media firms operating within the marketplace to produce content designed to attract advertisers' preferred audiences, particularly when advertising constitutes the majority of their revenue streams (Baker, *Media, Markets, and Democracy* 26; Napoli, *Audience Economics* 4; Turow, *Breaking Up America*). Turow argues that since the 1970s a shift has been taking place from mass marketing to audience segmentation, resulting in the rise of media products increasingly aimed at specific social segments (*Breaking Up America*). He maintains that media increasingly "signal" to audience members that they either do or do not belong in a particular audience by developing formats and brands deliberately designed to attract some segments and alienate others. Napoli also associates the rise of audience segmentation with more targeted content aimed at desired demographics (*Audience Economics* 97). Koschat and Putsis found that the magazine industry caters primarily to young and affluent audiences who constitute the most valuable demographic group for advertisers and nearly universally ignores less desirable groups, such as elderly men with average incomes (216, 230–31). These studies all point to the strong link between valued audiences and the types of media content produced.

Advertising-supported media are less likely to generate content that serves the preferences and interests of less valued audiences and may even take steps to exclude them from their audience pool. A number of studies confirm this assertion. Picard and Brody found that in the 1980s and 1990s, newspapers increasingly sought out smaller and more profitable audience segments, altering their subject matter and news content to appeal to more affluent readers and cutting circulation in high-cost areas or in areas that did not reach advertisers' desired demographics (89). These areas included urban ghettoes, minority communities, rural areas, and low-income districts.[8] The same study showed that it made economic sense for some newspapers to raise prices in order to reduce circulation and eliminate readers with undesirable demographics. In these cases, the revenues gained by offering advertisers more efficiently delivered upscale audiences, as well as the distribution costs saved by cutting circulation, offset the loss of a more sizeable and demographically varied audience. An earlier study by Thompson also found that newspapers could increase their profits by deliberately shrinking their readership in order to produce a more concentrated upscale audience that they could sell at a higher price to advertisers (262). Other studies show that the trade-off between gross circulation and a more valued, if smaller, audience demographic also applies to the magazine industry. Kalita and Ducoffe found that publications that earned the most from advertising revenue charged their readers more, not less, per copy, contradicting the accepted wisdom that greater advertising revenues result in cheaper cover prices for consumers (7). Instead, the authors found that magazines could increase their overall revenues by raising the price charged to readers, shedding less affluent audience members, and increasing advertising revenue for the remaining readership. While large audiences are generally worth more to advertisers, these studies show that audience characteristics can sometimes matter more than size to advertisers and advertising-supported media and that media do not care equally about the preferences of all audience members. Even when less valued audiences are willing and able to pay, advertisers are less likely to prefer content of interest to these audiences.

Another area in which advertiser interests can differ markedly from those of audiences has to do with the wider media environment. Advertisers have a vested interest in placing their ads in a message environment that creates positive, rather than negative, associations with their products. This might variously mean an environment that is not cluttered or degraded by surrounding content (Picard, *Economics and Financing* 124); that is not critical of advertisers, their products, or their worldview (Baker, *Advertising and a Democratic Press* 44; Baker, *Media, Markets, and Democracy* 25); and that avoids controversial, potentially offensive, or depressing subject matter (Bettig and Hall 96; Napoli, *Audience Economics* 24). Advertisers' desire to avoid media environments that are inhospitable to their products is understandable. Common sense and history suggest that advertisers will avoid programming that might reflect negatively on their messages. For example, advertisers have avoided programming on war and other tragedies.[9] Research also confirms the inverse—that advertisements are more positively received when ensconced in upbeat or comedic programming (Goldberg and Gorn; Petty et al.). It should come as no surprise that, given the importance of advertiser support, media would reduce or eliminate content that does not conform to advertiser interests. In his history of advertising, Barnouw argues that a good advertising environment requires that media content be supportive of business, promote an ethic of consumption, and even avoid entertaining people too well (114–15). Barnouw gives the fate of 1950s anthology drama series as an example (105–6). The anthology drama format passed out of existence despite its enormous popularity with audiences, due to withdrawal of advertiser support. Though the shows garnered extremely high ratings, they became unpopular with advertisers, who saw their dark moods and serious themes as an inhospitable climate for advertisements.[10] In a related vein, a *New England Journal of Medicine* study found that magazines relying heavily on cigarette advertising were significantly less likely to write about the dangers of smoking (Blum). In these cases, even if advertiser interests are contrary to the wants and needs of audiences, the media have strong incentives to honor the interests of advertisers.

Media that rely primarily on consumer support to finance their operations provide a partial, though imperfect, solution to the shortcomings of advertising-supported media. With direct payment or subscription media, consumers serve as the main source of revenue, signaling their preferences directly to the media according to their willingness to pay (Gomery 511; Napoli, *Audience Economics* 182; Picard, *Media Economics* 48). Consequently, consumer-supported media have no incentive to place the needs of advertisers before audiences. These media, which include books, a smattering of magazines, satellite radio, some premium cable channels, pay-per-view cable, and some Internet service providers (ISPs), can better serve the needs and interests of paying consumers. Yet, consumer-supported media have a downside. They link the availability of media entirely to the ability to pay. Baker notes that what people are willing to pay does not offer a comparative or equivalent measure of preferences, since unequal distribution of wealth gives the wealthy a greater ability to pay that does not denote stronger preferences (*Media, Markets, and Democracy* 72). In addition, research has shown that this model results in better access for those with higher incomes, as is the case with cable television and the Internet (Straubhaar and LaRose 305). The fact that access to subscription media correlates with income suggests that the consumer-supported media model may contribute to an information gap between those who can and those who cannot afford high-quality news and entertainment. This gap is highly problematic for democratic societies that rely on information and communication as a cornerstone of self-governance. In addition, the rise of subscription-based information and entertainment services carries with it the threat that as the more affluent consumers migrate to these private media enclaves, free or cheap advertiser-subsidized media options will become increasingly revenue starved and financially unviable. This outcome could further widen the gap between the information "haves" and "have-nots."

Stock Markets, Media Behavior, and Content

A media firm's status as a publicly traded company can also subject it to market pressures that systematically shape content in ways that are not always beneficial for audiences. Publicly traded companies enter the stock market in order to sell shares in their ownership and obtain capital for growth and development. Most major media companies are publicly owned and traded (Compaine and Gomery 491). Publicly traded companies must answer to the demands of the investment marketplace, whose chief concerns are profits and stock values, rather than the quality, diversity, or availability of media content. Investors buy shares in publicly traded media companies in order to receive a return on their investment. The value of their stocks, and ultimately their companies, is tied to quarterly earnings reports and the ability to meet analysts' estimates. Investors have short-term financial expectations that profits, margins, revenues, and stock values will increase. Investors, particularly large institutional investors, also have a great deal of power over the companies they own. If investors think that a company is not doing well financially, they can easily move their money to other investment opportunities, contributing further to the difficulties or devaluation of the company. Publicly traded companies internalize investors' expectations through a variety of incentives given to their management, board members, and key personnel. These incentives, which include bonuses and stock options or grants that depend on market performance, align the interests of company management with those of stockholders and are meant to ensure that companies act in the best interests of investors. For publicly traded media companies, investors are yet another interest to serve, and one that subjects them to an array of financial pressures and market imperatives that may be contrary to the interests of audiences.

Although U.S. media have always been commercial entities with primarily economic goals, publicly traded media companies may be especially inclined, or even compelled, to bring a commercial, rather than a public-service, orientation to their business (Picard, *Economics and Financing* 184; Shoemaker and Reese 121). Since the 1980s, newspapers have increasingly turned to the stock market as a source of capital. Cranberg, Bezanson, and Soloski found that publicly traded newspapers often improve financial performance in ways that compromise their historic role as sources of news and information in a democracy. Most of the papers they studied had primarily financial goals, and these goals were met by cutting personnel costs, hiring or retaining fewer and less experienced personnel, reducing the amount and quality of content carried, prioritizing content that caters to more valued audience segments, and cutting back on general circulation in order to better concentrate the valued audience and increase advertiser revenues (9, 11). Cranberg, Bezanson, and Soloski argue that these practices can compromise news content by impairing its quality and accuracy, eroding the traditional division between the news and business sides of newspapers, encouraging papers to produce news that panders to advertiser-preferred audience segments rather than news of interest or concern to the broader public, and decreasing editors' abilities to exercise their professional judgment due to strict financial controls (12–13). As Gans has found, many of these problems are already endemic in broadcast-television news organizations that feel pressure to increase profitability (*Democracy and the News; Deciding What's News*).[11] Cranberg, Bezanson, and Soloski concluded that publicly traded newspapers privilege the interests of stockholders and advertisers over those of the local communities whose residents they are supposed to serve (87, 106). Atkin and Litman found that the need to place profits over audience interests is also a factor in broadcasting, where networks cancel higher-rated programs with small profit margins or high production costs over lower-rated programs that are more profitable overall, and where networks choose to air reruns over original programming because the savings on production costs make up for losses in advertising revenue (33–34). While private media owners may behave similarly, they at least have more flexibility to pursue long-term interests, audience concerns, or their own editorial judgment (Compaine and Gomery 490).

New Media, Markets, and Industry Concentration

New media will not inevitably solve the problems of old media. Neoliberal policy analysts like Fowler and Brenner argue that more outlets result in greater content diversity and allow markets to better satisfy consumer needs (209–10). New media and the liberalization of media industries have produced more outlets for media content and greater competition between substitutable media like broadcast and cable television. Yet, there is little reason to believe that the shortcomings of the media market will not affect these new outlets. New or more technology does not change the facts that media markets cater overwhelmingly to valued audience segments, ignore or exclude undervalued audiences, tailor content first and foremost to the needs of advertisers, or privilege profit making above the quality and diversity of their products. Marketplace imperatives determine these practices. In fact, new technologies and increased competition could exacerbate, rather than alleviate, the shortcomings that accompany market driven media.

The proliferation of media outlets could enable the development of some new and original content, but increasing audience fragmentation may temper the quality and diversity of this content. More channels and increased intermedia competition creates opportunities to carve the audience up into smaller and smaller audience segments. Increased audience segmentation will allow media to create some new content, though they are likely to continue aiming this content at valued audience segments. In addition, as the audience spreads itself out over a greater number of outlets, each outlet attracts ever smaller fragments of the available audience. Napoli points out that fragmentation, along with the greater autonomy afforded by new technologies and services like video on demand, personal video recorders, and the Internet, makes it harder to measure, and thus monetize, audiences. Smaller audience numbers make measurement data less reliable, and some audience numbers may even be too small to register with ratings services ("Internet" 8; *Audience Economics* 90). The diminishing audience size for any one outlet and the difficulties with measuring or predicting audience behavior makes it a less valuable commodity for advertisers. As a result, fragmented audiences garner less revenue for content providers.

Increased competition among outlets and more outlets overall do not translate simply into more diverse or higher-quality content. Atkin and Litman found that network television's response to revenue losses caused by competition from cable television and videocassette recorders in the 1970s and 1980s was to program less original programming, or more reruns (42). This response was rational given that any losses in advertising revenue could be made up in savings in production costs. Rogers and Woodbury also argue that market economics can support only a certain amount of diversity. They found that large increases in the number of local radio stations in a market do not significantly increase the diversity of program formats (90). Rather, markets could support only a limited number of local radio stations.

Finally, despite the growth of media outlets, media market concentration may result in fewer voices. Media concentration enables fewer and fewer companies to control the nation's media. Long-term trends toward market concentration in U.S. media are significant. The number of U.S. cities with two or more daily newspapers has declined from 502 in 1923 to 19 in 1996 (Compaine and Gomery 9). Only a handful of the biggest cities have more than one newspaper (Gans, *Democracy and the News* 22), and the local daily newspaper market is highly concentrated (Picard, *Media Economics* 34). According to the Herfindahl-Hirschmann Index, the television broadcasting market is moderately concentrated (Compaine and Gomery 558), and concentration in the radio industry has doubled between 1992 and 1997 (Drushel).[12] Cable operators in most cities have no direct competitors, and the ten largest cable multisystem operators reach nearly 50 percent of all television households (Compaine and Gomery 485). In the 1980s, fifty corporations dominated the major mass media, while twenty years later that number shrunk to six (Bagdikian xx–xxi). Industry concentration is likely to continue as companies seek greater economies of scope and scale, as technological developments create new opportunities for convergence, and as regulatory barriers against industry consolidation fall. Concentration may have a variety of negative effects of content. Some studies have found that when local newspaper markets moved from competitive to monopoly market structures, diversity and local news coverage suffered (Donohue and Glasser; Grotta; Lacy; and Rarick and Hartman). Others have linked market concentration in television with a lack of diversity of content and program types (Dominick and Pearce; Fox et al.; Golding and Middleton; Valdez; and Westen). In addition, industry concentration permits a diminishing number of media firms to determine content decisions. In a legal setting where defensive speech rights prevail, a paucity of media firms can also claim exclusive rights to speak over their media and prevent other voices from gaining access. Firm owners and managers also have the power to define the overall goals and scope of their companies and to determine the deployment of resources (Murdock 122–23). They need not intervene directly in the daily operations of their companies in order to shape or control media content. Fewer firms signify that fewer people may have the right or ready ability to have their voices heard.

Democratic Communication in a Representational Democracy

Some might object to the argument that citizens of democratic societies require widespread social mediation and media access on the basis that modern nations have opted to institute representative, rather than direct, democracies. Unlike the ancient Greeks, who professed a democratic ideal in which citizens would participate directly in every political decision made, today's nation-states adhere to a democratic system in which citizens elect officials who represent their views and interests in political matters. Representational politics enables nations with vast territories and populations to enact democracy on a large scale. If democracy today is representative, why should we adhere to a more participatory standard of communication?

There are several answers to this question. First, representation is a compromise position that, while serving the needs of large, modern democracies, falls short of the ideal for which democrats strive. Representation promotes efficiency by allowing a small number of elected representatives to govern in all public matters all the time (Barber xxii). In addition, representation promotes accountability because elected officials who depend on citizens' votes are more likely to serve their interests. Yet, representational politics effectively alienates individuals from their role as self-governing citizens, removing them from active and ongoing participation in the political process. This reduced form of participation, which limits citizens to listening, thinking, and voting for representatives, is a weak version of democracy. While it may be pragmatic and practicable, it is not the ideal. In fact, Dahl notes the discrepancy between the real and ideal practice of democracy in advanced "democratic" countries and argues that the goal of democracies should be to close this gap by moving toward greater political participation (177, 219). One way to do so is to develop and strengthen the institutions and resources necessary for a more democratic society, including opportunities to engage in political discussion, set agendas, and obtain information. For those who believe in democracy, a representative system is a necessary compromise that does not and should not preclude the development of more participatory practices and institutions.

In addition, the moral justification of democracy rests on the principles that people are equally qualified to govern themselves and that each person is the best judge of their own interests, as well as the common good. Democracy asserts that everyone, rather than a select few, has the capacity to govern and that self-governance leads to better outcomes than alternative forms of politics based on guardianship. The democratic faith in individuals to make good decisions in the common interest presumes that everyone has equal and adequate opportunities to make their own interests known, to discover the common interest, and to express their preferences in the political arena. This holds true whether people govern themselves directly or by proxy. Consequently, democratic societies need appropriate resources and institutions to support the development of an informed and knowledgeable citizenry. The more a democracy can support people's ability to know and make known the common good, the closer it moves toward the democratic ideal. This goal becomes all the more important when the majority of our political institutions are representational. Definitions of speech rights that support democratic communication can help ensure that citizens find opportunities to create and attain social knowledge and tie representational politics to strong democratic moorings.

Fortunately, communication technology presents the opportunity to overcome obstacles to democratic communication caused by the large scale of modern nation-states. As long as law does not preclude it, democratic societies can use existing communications technology to augment political participation. As Barber notes, the modern democratic problem of scale is largely a problem of communication (247–48). Because political communities are human associations bound by communication, politics enacted at the level of nation-states requires methods of communication that help citizens identify and understand their collective interests on a concomitant scale. Media are particularly important resources in large-scale societies where the size of the population makes unmediated, face-to-face communication among the entire demos impossible. While it is unfeasible to expect that every citizen have direct access to all media, the media system as a whole could allow everyone access to some communication resources at least some of the time.

Conclusion

An empowering approach to speech rights allows the government to affirmatively support the conditions conducive to democratic communication. While markets may behave efficiently and allocate resources according to the interests of important market participants, markets alone cannot fulfill all the needs of democratic societies. Media markets cannot guarantee the production of diverse and high-quality goods and services aimed at meeting the communication needs of all citizens. In fact, efficient market behavior systematically favors the interests of advertisers, shareholders, and more valued audience segments over those of the broader populace, including the poor, the very young and old, and racial and ethnic minorities. Media markets also systematically disfavor unpopular and minority viewpoints—two things that liberal democrats of all stripes agree are essential components of democratic communication. These shortcomings are alarming to those who view information and communication as an essential democratic resource. The defensive approach to speech rights, which mandates only that the government refrain from action, is powerless to mitigate these problems. Yet, in a democracy, it is not unreasonable for citizens to look to government to correct for market behavior that is rational but does not serve their interests. When the public's interest in democratic communication conflicts with commercial goals and values, it is the government's responsibility to intervene to establish more democratic conditions. By saying that the government has a roll in mitigating the shortcomings of media markets in democratic societies, I do not mean to suggest that the government should control media or that media markets should be abandoned altogether. Rather, we should recognize, as Mulgan does, that both markets and governments have their own goals and method of operating and that neither has a monopoly on how to best produce information goods (261). Therefore, when markets fail to produce socially desirable outcomes, government regulation designed to produce more speech opportunities is justified.

In this chapter, I examine contrasting interpretations of speech rights within modern liberal-democratic thinking. The defensive approach is the logical outgrowth of neoliberal political theory. From this perspective, the absence of oppression, private realms of action, and prohibitions on state action protect people's speech rights against society. The empowering approach stems from participatory-democratic theory, which argues that rights are social claims, protected through society, that allow people freedoms that do not otherwise exist. Freedom is a positive ability and capacity, as well as a shield against oppressive forces. Moreover, under the empowering framework, the state is an instrument of the public with a mandate to ensure the presence of public realms of action and the power to protect democratic communication from the social, political, and economic conditions that threaten its livelihood.

Participatory-democratic theory redefines the terms of liberal discourse and offers a comprehensive analysis of political life that serves as a useful corrective to the neoliberal worldview. At the heart of the participatory-democratic approach is a commitment to extend and strengthen democratic processes throughout society. This theory provides a firm foundation from which to formulate the basic criteria for speech rights in a democracy. Accordingly, empowering speech rights require the ability to send and receive information and the existence of public communicative spaces. In the remainder of this book, I examine whether and to what extent U.S. law and policy recognize empowering speech rights in practice, the obstacles confronting their fuller realization in the future, and the options available to effect a more democratic interpretation of speech rights.

3 Social Mediation in Print and Broadcast Media

THE SUPREME COURT ESTABLISHED current law on the right to send and receive communication in print and broadcast within a brief five-year span. The determining cases came at the height of a grassroots citizens' movement for media access. This movement sought to make the media more responsive and responsible in their role as social mediators within democratic societies. Arguing that street corners and public parks were no longer the most relevant sites for participation in public discourse, members of the movement pressed for a right of access to the mass media.[1] Throughout North America, access advocates sought to create speaking opportunities in the visible and pervasive media of their era, namely print and broadcasting.

Members of the movement typically invoked what I have termed an empowering view of speech rights. Like participatory-democratic theorists, access advocates argued that meaningful speech rights must include both the right to send and receive communication through the dominant media, or what sympathetic legal scholars termed a right of access to the press and a right to know.[2] In 1967, Jerome Barron published a seminal article for the movement, titled "Access to the Press—A New First Amendment Right." In it, Barron outlined an argument, and reviewed precedents, to support an essentially empowering interpretation of the First Amendment. Barron argued that the marketplace theory of speech rights is romantic and outdated because the real conditions of commercial media markets fail to support speech rights. According to Barron, commercial media are economically compelled to cater to large audiences, to avoid offending advertisers, and to refrain from airing controversial or unpopular ideas that might adversely affect their business (1646). Their chief concern is profits, not the production of news and information vital to democratic processes. Without a constitutional right of access, speech rights would be a reality for media owners, but not for the vast majority who lack opportunities to speak in the dominant media of their era. The First Amendment, said Barron, should support speech opportunities in all media with a social impact or public function. Since both print and broadcast media influence democratic publics and supply them with essential news and information, both are quasipublic in nature and both compel affirmative government protection and promotion of speech rights.

The cases that set the speech regimes for print and broadcast—*Red Lion Broadcasting v. FCC, Columbia Broadcasting System v. Democratic National Committee,* and *Miami Herald v. Tornillo*—were fought over policies that sought to create limited opportunities for the public to speak in the media. All of these policies, whether they focused on media access, content diversity, a multiplicity of information sources, or opportunities to reply to media attacks, involved a right to engage in social mediation and a vision of public communicative space. One question facing the Court was whether the First Amendment required and could sanction policies that created opportunities to speak through the media. In addition, the policies raised questions of public space in two ways. First, they implied that the media had a public role to play in democratic life, and, second, they attempted to privilege processes related to democratic decision-making in media that are largely privately controlled. Nevertheless, the Court addressed the public-space dimensions of these cases indirectly, if at all. Instead, it framed each case as being about the public's right to either send or receive communication. Close analyses of these cases show how empowering and defensive views of democratic communication lead alternately to the negation or affirmation of the public's right to engage in social mediation.

The Right to Receive in Broadcast: The Ambivalent Treatment of Speech Rights in Red Lion

In *Red Lion,* the Supreme Court was asked to determine the constitutionality of federal communication policies promoting the public's right to send and receive balanced information. The case involved the FCC's now defunct Fairness Doctrine, which required that broadcasters air fair coverage of controversial issues of public importance (U.S. FCC, "Fairness Doctrine"). Also under scrutiny were two rules closely related to the Fairness Doctrine, which mandated that broadcasters give a right of reply to the subjects of personal or political attacks (*Red Lion* 373–75).[3] The doctrine and its corollaries asserted a limited claim on behalf of the public for speech rights in broadcasting. The FCC had designed these policies to ensure that broadcasters fostered informed public opinions, promoted "freedom of speech . . . for the people of the Nation as a whole," and refrained from imposing restraints on the public's speech rights (U.S. FCC, "Report on Editorializing" 1248–49).

The fairness rules invoked, but did not fully embrace, a public right to engage in social mediation. While the Fairness Doctrine supported the public's right to receive information, it did not require that citizens have actual opportunities to speak over the airwaves. Broadcasters could satisfy their fairness obligations by speaking on behalf of the public. The doctrine did not support access to the media or the ability of people to speak for themselves. The personal-attack and political-editorializing rules, on the other hand, claimed that certain members of the public should be able to communicate through the broadcast medium. These rules created a narrowly drawn right of reply that invoked both a right to send and receive communication.

Red Lion was the result of two challenges to the fairness rules. One challenge involved the Red Lion Broadcasting Company. Red Lion's station, WGCB in Pennsylvania, had aired a program in which a Christian minister attacked author Fred J. Cook for his contributions to the left-wing journal *The Nation* and denigrated his then-recent book on Barry Goldwater (*Red Lion* 372–73). After WGCB refused Cook the opportunity to reply to these attacks, he took his case to the FCC, which determined that the station's refusal violated the personal-attack rules of the Fairness Doctrine. When a U.S. court of appeals affirmed both the FCC order and the Fairness Doctrine as constitutional, Red Lion Broadcasting petitioned the Supreme Court to overturn the decision. The other case involved a direct challenge, brought by the Radio Television News Directors Association, to the FCC's 1967 rule on personal attacks and political editorializing. This time, a U.S. court of appeals struck down the rules as a violation of broadcasters' speech rights, and the government appealed. The Supreme Court heard both cases together.

The central question before the Supreme Court in *Red Lion* was whether the public has speech rights in privately controlled, though publicly owned, broadcast media. In a unanimous decision, the Supreme Court declared the Fairness Doctrine and its associated rules constitutionally sound. The Court offered two reasons for its decision. First, Congress had authorized the FCC to implement reasonable rules and regulations in the public interest. Second, the doctrine and its component rules served to enhance rather than to abridge the First Amendment rights of the public and the press (*Red Lion* 375). The Court also linked its decision to spectrum scarcity, arguing that the paucity of broadcast opportunities on a publicly held resource, as well as government licensing of that resource, necessitates that the public retain some First Amendment rights in broadcasting (30). Textbook readings of the case attribute the *Red Lion* decision primarily to the Court's perception of spectrum scarcity (Gillmor, Barron, and Simon 676; Middleton, Chamberlin, and Bunker 527). Yet, spectrum scarcity can count as a factor only after the Court decides that the real conditions in broadcasting are relevant to its analysis of speech rights. Indeed, a closer reading of the case suggests that the *Red Lion* decision is not simply motivated by spectrum scarcity, but rather by a particular philosophy of democratic communication. In setting forth its opinion, the Court made use of several tenets of participatory-democratic theory. The Court maintained that the government may act affirmatively to promote speech rights, that nongovernmental actors are capable of coercion, and that the real conditions influencing speech opportunities are relevant to determinations of speech rights.

The Court rejected the contention that all state action constitutes censorship. In the case of broadcasting, the Court argued, government regulation promotes speech rights in several ways. First and foremost, government regulation and rationalization of broadcast spectrum is a necessary prerequisite to the effective use of the medium (*Red Lion* 376). Without the government regulation of otherwise chaotic spectrum space, no one would be able to speak or be heard over the airwaves. Additionally, regulations like the Fairness Doctrine crafted an appropriate balance between the speech rights of broadcasters and the public. According to the Court, the public status of the airwaves, as well as the government's role in allocating licenses, bestowed speech rights on the broader public. By allocating licenses while simultaneously requiring license holders to act as fiduciaries or trustees who adhere to public-interest regulations, the government was thought to preserve and promote the speech rights of all parties. Finally, the Court made a distinction between government policies that enhance and those that inhibit free speech. The fairness rules enhanced speech rights by ensuring that the public received balanced information on controversial issues without proscribing or prescribing any specific broadcast content (396).

The Court also argued that the government could act to protect the public's speech rights from infringement by private, nongovernmental censors. Citing *Associated Press v. US* (1945), a case that supported government sanctions against private actors who obstructed freedom of expression, the Court noted that broadcasters' speech rights did not include "a right to snuff out the free speech of others" (*Red Lion* 388). The Court said, "There is no sanctuary in the First Amendment for unlimited private censorship operating in a medium not open to all. Freedom of the press from governmental interference under the First Amendment does not sanction repression of that freedom by private interests" (*Associated Press,* cited in *Red Lion* 393). *Red Lion* recognized the ability of private actors to obstruct the speech rights of others, as well as the responsibility of the government to protect the public's rights against the coercive power of broadcasters (390).

Finally, the *Red Lion* Court was willing, albeit in a limited manner, to acknowledge the real-world conditions in which broadcast speech operates and to interpret speech rights in light of these conditions. The Court granted limited speech rights to those who are denied a license to utilize a scarce public resource subject to technical market failure (*Red Lion* 399–400). The Court reasoned that as long as the government is in the position to grant broadcast licenses to some while denying others, fairness policies are justifiable. The Court explicitly declined to consider whether other types of market failure might necessitate the protection of public speech rights in the broadcast media (401, no. 28). Yet, its assertion that speech rights must be determined in light of the context of scarce, government-licensed spectrum space resonates with an empowering approach to speech rights.

Despite its empowering elements, the *Red Lion* decision did not offer unmitigated support to empowering speech rights. *Red Lion* did insist on the First Amendment rights of viewers and listeners to receive information, but it made no mention of the right to send information. The Court affirmed the public's right to be informed but not the right of access to the media necessary to enable effective social mediation. *Red Lion* assumed, as Owen (25) pointed out, that a government policy that simulates free expression by prodding broadcasters to speak as representatives for the broader public adequately protects speech rights. Though it upheld the personal-attack and political-editorializing rules, which created limited access to the airwaves under certain circumstances, the Court sidestepped recognition of a right to send information or to represent one's own views. The Court said only that the FCC has the authority to enact rules compatible with the First Amendment goal of fostering an informed public, that the fairness rules are not incompatible with this goal, and that any rights of access are a matter of FCC discretion.

The Right to Send in Broadcast: The Defensive Framework of CBS v. DNC

Red Lion confirmed that the public, and not just the broadcast licensee, has speech rights in broadcasting. Nevertheless, the Court upheld the fairness rules on the basis of a right to receive information only, not on the right to send it. Even though some of the rules guaranteed certain people the ability to represent their views in the media, the Court did not determine whether speech rights necessarily also included a right to speak. Once Red Lion declared the public's speech rights in broadcasting, however, it was only a matter of time until someone raised the question of whether these rights require an affirmative ability to send information over the airwaves.

In 1970, the year following Red Lion, two citizens' groups asked the FCC to sanction a right to speak as part of the public's speech rights in broadcasting. The Business Executives' Move for Vietnam Peace approached the FCC after a failed attempt to place an editorial advertisement against the Vietnam War on a Washington, D.C., radio station. The station, WTOP, had a blanket policy against selling advertising time to anyone who wanted to express controversial views. That same year, the Democratic National Committee told the FCC that neither CBS nor ABC was willing to sell it television airtime for a half-hour program that addressed members of the Democratic Party (Democratic National Committee 216–17). Both the Business Executives' Move for Vietnam Peace and the Democratic National Committee thought their speech rights had been violated. In their view, all responsible members of the public deserved some right of access to commercial time slots that broadcasters routinely made available to advertisers and others to convey their messages. In its rulings on these cases, the FCC determined that fairness obligations required broadcasters to represent community views but did not entail a public right of access in broadcasting (Democratic National Committee 224; Business Executives' Move for Vietnam Peace 242–43). In 1971, a U.S. court of appeals reversed the FCC ruling, holding that flat bans on editorial advertisements did violate the public's speech rights (Business Executives' Move for Vietnam Peace v. FCC). The appeals court argued that the public's speech rights necessarily include an expressive dimension that paternalistic policies that allow broadcasters alone to speak cannot satisfy.[4]

CBS v. DNC reached the U.S. Supreme Court in 1973. The central question raised, according to the Court, was whether broadcaster policies against selling airtime for issue advertising violated either the First Amendment or the 1934 Communications Act. In answering this question, the Court sought to balance what it saw as the conflicting First Amendment interests of broadcasters and the public. The *CBS v. DNC* Court said that *Red Lion* gave the public a right to be informed, not to speak—a right of access to ideas, not to airwaves. An arrangement that limits the public's speech rights to a right to receive information and gives broadcasters editorial rights to decide who may speak maintains an optimal balance between public and private speech rights. Furthermore, the Court argued that Congress had always favored the mix of public and private control in broadcasting represented by the status quo arrangement (*CBS v. DNC* 105–6). The 1934 Communications Act made broadcasters public trustees with both journalistic freedom and public-interest obligations. In this way, the government could ask broadcasters to serve the public without subjecting them to government censorship. Additionally, neither the legislative history nor the 1934 Communications Act supported an individual right of access. In the Court's view, Congress had already rejected that idea when they rejected a common-carrier model for broadcast regulation. Policies like the Fairness Doctrine arose, said the Court, to finesse the intended public-private balance by mandating fair and adequate coverage of controversial issues while allowing broadcasters editorial discretion over how to achieve these objectives.

The Court denied that broadcaster policies violated the First Amendment. The First Amendment, noted the Court, applies to government action, not to private actors. In the Court's view, there is no state action present in broadcasting because the actions of licensees do not constitute government action.[5] Broadcasters are journalistic free agents bound only by their duties as public trustees, and the FCC's relationship to broadcasters is one of an "overseer," "arbiter," or "guardian" (*CBS v. DNC* 118). Moreover, a finding of state action would overturn the delicate balance between private control and public obligation in broadcasting. The government cannot compromise broadcasters' editorial control over media access and at the same time hold them accountable for what appears on the airwaves. Absolute control over all broadcast speech was necessary, the Court reasoned, for fairness policies to work. Finally, the Court accepted the FCC's claim that access policies would harm, rather than enhance, free speech. The right to buy paid advertising time would allow the wealthy to unduly influence the political agenda. It would jeopardize the effectiveness of the Fairness Doctrine by stripping editorial control away from broadcasters who are accountable and subjecting the public to self-appointed commentators who are not. Lastly, it would risk greater government control over broadcast content by drawing the government into day-to-day decision-making about who deserves access. While the *CBS v. DNC* Court determined that the First Amendment did not require a right to speak in broadcasting, it did not rule out the possibility that the government might adopt some acceptable right of access for future media. In fact, the Court pointed to the rise of cable television, recent federal policy requiring cable operators to offer public-access channels, and the ability of new technologies to resolve access problems as reasons not to upset the regulatory status quo in broadcasting (*CBS v. DNC* 132).

A defensive stream of logic flowed alongside the Court's express rationale in the case. The Court's composition had changed dramatically since *Red Lion,* and this change was evident in both the substance and the philosophical framework of the *CBS v. DNC* decision. While *Red Lion* was decided by the liberal Warren Court and authored by Kennedy appointee Byron White, *CBS v. DNC* was heard by the more conservative Burger Court and authored by Burger himself, a Nixon appointee. The *CBS v. DNC* Court denied the defendants the right to represent themselves in the broadcast media, using a defensive approach to contain the empowering implications of *Red Lion.* Although it accepted the idea of public speech rights in broadcast, the Court explicitly limited their scope to the right to receive information. A right to receive, said the Court, gave sufficient protection to the public's interest in being informed about controversial issues. Ultimately, the decision bifurcated the conjoint aspects of social mediation, severing the right to send from the right to receive in broadcast.

The Court did not consider self-expression and self-representation to be integral elements of the public's speech rights. Nor did it take a participatory view of political or social knowledge. For the *CBS v. DNC* Court, social knowledge is something that broadcasters could simply represent to the public, not something that has to be community generated. Rather, control over the treatment of public issues is best left to the broadcaster. The Court stated, "We [cannot] accept the . . . view that every potential speaker is 'the best judge' of what the listening public ought to hear or indeed the best judge of the merits of his or her views. All journalistic tradition and experience is to the contrary. For better or worse, editing is what editors are for; and editing is selection and choice of material. That editors—newspaper or broadcast—can and do abuse this power is beyond doubt, but that is no reason to deny the discretion Congress provided. Calculated risks of abuse are taken in order to preserve higher values" (*CBS v. DNC* 125–26). In the Court's view, the public's right to represent itself has little value. Though willing to risk the results of exclusive broadcaster control of the medium, the Court is not willing to risk the outcome of narrowly drawn policies allowing members of the public to represent themselves and their views.

For the Court, government action is the principal and prime threat to speech rights in broadcast. The Court saw the choice over whether to uphold access policies as a choice between government censorship and private suppression of speech. The Court argued that Congress feared the pervasive and uncontrollable nature of government censorship more than it feared private actors, a view reflected in the First Amendment's prohibition on government action exclusively (*CBS v. DNC* 106). Private censorship by broadcast licensees is acceptable as long as the licensee adequately covers important public issues. Government policies that create limited rights of access to broadcasting, however, are examples of impermissible government interference. In this logic, unencumbered broadcaster speech is equated with freedom, while a government policy allowing the public limited opportunities to speak is seen as infringing on the speech rights of broadcasters (121–22).

Finally, neither *CBS v. DNC* nor *Red Lion* recognized or protected public space in broadcasting. In the United States, policies that promote a right of access or a right to receive in effect create pockets of democratic public space in media otherwise organized along private-market principles. Yet, both Courts overlooked obvious linkages between understandings of the broadcast medium and public-forum law, or the law governing public spaces. Public-forum law, which applies to all public property designated for communicative purposes, protects public speech rights from both government and private censors. At the time these cases were decided, public-forum law strongly suggested that the public had speech rights wherever particularly close relations between government and private actors existed and on private property that possessed a public character or function (*Burton v. Wilmington Parking Authority* [1961]; *Amalgamated Food Employees Union Local 590 v. Logan Valley Plaza* [1968]; and *Marsh v. Alabama* [1946]). Both the *CBS v. DNC* and *Red Lion* Courts acknowledged that broadcast spectrum was public property and that the government licensing process allowed some people to speak at the expense of others. Yet, neither wanted to analyze broadcasting in relation to public-forum law or draw the inevitable conclusion that broadcasting did indeed have a public function and character. In fact, one member of the *CBS v. DNC* Court worried that were public-forum law to be applied, broadcasting might be transformed into an entirely open medium (140–41). The studious deflection of the public-space question may reflect the endemic difficulty of imagining or creating public spaces in privately operated media in U.S. law.

While the majority opinion dismissed the public's right to send information, a dissent written by Justice Brennan and joined by Justice Marshall,
adopted an empowering framework to argue that the Court's decision is
entirely contrary to the meaning and purpose of the First Amendment. For
Brennan, the underlying conflict centered on "the people's right to engage
in and to hear vigorous public debate on the broadcast media"(*CBS v. DNC*
173). Brennan argued that any balance of the speech rights of broadcasters
and the broader public must allow the public some right to participate in, as
well as to receive, broadcast communication. Although broadcasters have a
legitimate interest in editing broadcast content, they do not have an overrid-
ing right to control all content. By upholding policies that foreclose public
access to broadcasting, the majority opinion sacrificed a limited right of all
to speak in the dominant communications forum of the era to the absolute
right of broadcasters to monopolize speech in this forum.

Brennan maintained that speech rights must include a right of access to
the airwaves and that the Fairness Doctrine is no substitute for this right.
Red Lion had affirmed the public's speech rights in broadcasting, and Supreme Court precedents suggested that a right to receive information alone
could not satisfy the public's speech rights, as the majority opinion held.
The Supreme Court, said Brennan, often recognized the close relationship
between diverse viewpoints and open forums for communication. In fact,
the Court recognized that a central purpose of the First Amendment was to
ensure "uninhibited, robust, and wideopen" public debate and to protect
"the widest possible dissemination of information from diverse and antagonistic sources" (*Associated Press* 20, cited in *CBS v. DNC* 184). The Fairness
Doctrine by itself could not fulfill these purposes:

> The Court's reliance on the Fairness Doctrine as the *sole* means of informing
> the public seriously misconceives and underestimates the public's interest in
> receiving ideas and information directly from the advocates of those ideas
> without the interposition of journalistic middlemen. Under the Fairness
> Doctrine, broadcasters decide what issues are "important," how "fully" to
> cover them, and what format, time and style of coverage are "appropriate."
> The retention of such *absolute* control in the hands of a few Government li-
> censees is inimical to the First Amendment, for vigorous, free debate can be
> attained only when members of the public have at least *some* opportunity to
> take the initiative and editorial control into their own hands. (*CBS v. DNC*
> 189–90, emphasis original)

Although the Fairness Doctrine protects the public's interest in receiving
information, it does not facilitate self-expression. The government cannot

alienate self-expression, an integral aspect of speech rights, from the individual and vest it with the broadcaster. Allowing the broadcaster to act as a representative for various viewpoints within a community and to maintain near total control over the coverage of controversial issues does not serve the public's speech rights. Rather, some opportunities for the public to gain access to the airwaves, to raise issues, and to frame the presentation of their own views are necessary to ensure legitimate public debate and cultivate an informed citizenry.

Finally, Brennan recognized the public character and function of broadcasting. First, he argued that the Court could not deny the extraordinarily close relationship that exists between broadcasting and government action. The public status of the airwaves, the government-conferred license to broadcast, extensive federal regulation of broadcasting, and the FCC's approval of the disputed fairness policies are sufficient evidence of state action in broadcasting under the Court's own precedents (*CBS v. DNC* 174). Brennan argued that government involvement in broadcasting necessitates that First Amendment restraints apply to broadcasters, implicitly analogizing broadcasting with public forums (182). In broadcasting, said Brennan, the First Amendment should prohibit both the government and broadcasters from infringing on the public's speech rights. Furthermore, broadcasting has a public function. The broadcast media are the country's prime source of news and information. Brennan pointed out that the speech rights of the public signify little if they do not guarantee a right of access in the dominant media. He said, "Although 'full and free discussion' of ideas may have been a reality in the heyday of political pamphleteering, modern technological developments in the field of communications have made the soapbox orator and the leafleteer virtually obsolete. And, in light of the current dominance of the electronic media as the most effective means of reaching the public, any policy that absolutely denies citizens access to the airwaves necessarily renders even the concept of 'full and free discussion' practically meaningless" (197). For Brennan, the public's speech rights require a right to send information, as well as to receive it, and public spaces in which to actualize those rights.

Definitively Defensive: Social Mediation in Print

The Supreme Court decided the status of the right to participate in social mediation in print in *Miami Herald v. Tornillo*. In *Miami Herald,* the Court examined the constitutionality of a Florida statute that gave political candidates a direct right of reply to newspapers who had maligned them during an election.[6] The statute invoked the right of citizens to receive information about political candidates during an election and the rights of candidates to provide information about themselves and their candidacy. Pat Tornillo, a candidate for the Florida House of Representatives, brought the case against the *Miami Herald* after the paper published two scathing editorials against him and refused him the opportunity to reply, a clear violation of the statute. The case served as a testing ground for a theory of media access advanced by Tornillo's lawyer, Jerome Barron. In *Miami Herald,* Barron argued that the government should enforce the Florida statute as a means of safeguarding fair elections, an informed electorate, and the dissemination of information about important public issues (Brief for Appellee Pat L. Tornillo Jr.).

Although the Supreme Court had upheld the Fairness Doctrine in broadcasting, it unanimously rejected the Florida statute as a violation of the First Amendment rights of the print media. The Court gave several reasons for its decision. First, the justices stated that compelling newspapers "to publish that which 'reason' tells them should not be published" is no different from censoring newspaper content (*Miami Herald* 257). Both acts, said the Court, were impermissible restraints on free speech. Second, the Court viewed the statute as a content-based restriction on the free-press rights of newspapers that might cause newspapers to avoid potentially controversial speech, inducing a so-called "chilling effect" (258). Third, the Court claimed that the statute authorized an unconstitutional intrusion on the function of newspaper editors (259). A free press must be allowed to determine content, slant, and length of newspaper coverage.

Though ostensibly guided by legal absolutism, or the literal interpretation of the First Amendment, which insists that Congress shall simply "make no law" regulating speech, the *Miami Herald* Court makes use of a broadly defensive approach to speech rights. The Court rejected the claim that an economically based scarcity of speech opportunities justified government intervention (Barron and Dienes 393; Van Alstyne 86). The justices reviewed the arguments of Tornillo, the appellee, including the charges that the newspaper industry had become monopolistic, anticompetitive, and highly concentrated; that entry into the newspaper market was prohibitively expensive; and that citizens generally lacked the means to participate in contemporary public debate (*Miami Herald* 250–54). After recounting these arguments at length, the Court quickly disposed of them in its subsequent analysis.[7] Whether these conditions prevailed, said the Court, had no bearing on considerations of speech rights because any corrective mechanism necessarily involved government coercion.

The *Miami Herald* Court categorically dismissed government remedies as legitimate solutions to scarce speaking opportunities in the newspaper market. According to the Court, such solutions were preempted by the fact that government action and government coercion are synonymous. It said, "The implementation of a remedy such as an enforceable right of access necessarily calls for some mechanism, either governmental or consensual. If it is governmental coercion, this at once brings about a confrontation with the express provisions of the First Amendment and the judicial gloss on that Amendment" (*Miami Herald* 255). Given its conflation of government regulation with coercion, the Court could not recognize the critical distinction made in *Red Lion* between government actions that abridge or enhance speech rights. For the *Miami Herald* Court, a press left to the exigencies of the marketplace, no matter how imperfect, was preferable to inherently coercive government policies.

In addition, while the *Red Lion* Court had considered the First Amendment rights of both the public and broadcasters, the *Miami Herald* Court addressed those of newspapers only. The Florida statue had suggested a view of speech rights that included the right of political candidates to provide information about their candidacy, the right of citizens to receive a range of information about candidates, and the authority of the government to promote fair elections and an informed electorate. However, rather than evaluate the multiple speech interests involved or attempt to craft a balance between potentially conflicting interests, the *Miami Herald* Court focused its attention on the speech rights of newspapers (244). As long as the newspaper was left alone, speech rights were operative. The Court's myopia was made possible by its belief that in the absence of government coercion the rights of all parties were adequately protected.

Conclusion

From the standpoint of First Amendment law, there are two important questions to ask about media-access policies. First: should the First Amendment allow, or require, democratic societies to provide opportunities for media access? Second: do specific access policies fit within acceptable First Amendment interpretations? In this book, I am primarily concerned with the first question. Given the need for social mediation in democratic societies, First Amendment law must not place a blanket prohibition on all access initiatives. Rather, the First Amendment must permit, and should even encourage, some degree of public access if the media is to serve as a resource for democratic communication. The second question asks the courts to assess the constitutionality of how specific policies implement access. Important questions for policy-makers include to whom should a right of access adhere and who should control or manage it. Unfortunately, there are no "one size fits all" answers to these questions. Access might justifiably take different forms on single-channel and multichannel media, within different media markets, or at different moments in history. Furthermore, the precise policies that can best support democratic communication at a given moment are a matter for experimental determination. While there is no singularly valid formula for mandating access, we must nevertheless consider the constitutionality of specific policies. These policies should be narrowly tailored to serve the government's interest in promoting democratic speech and should offer content-neutral speech opportunities without advancing a preferred government viewpoint.

The cases examined here provided two alternative models of media access. Policies like the Fairness Doctrine, the personal-attack and political-editorializing rules, and rights of reply for political candidates created narrowly tailored access opportunities for those whose views and interests were the objects of media bias. People seeking access could ask the print and broadcast media to honor these policies. If the media ignored their requests, they could appeal to the FCC or the courts to enforce the rules. Although the media's content triggered access rights, the policies themselves did not censor the media, but instead asked them to counterbalance their biases by disseminating additional speech. The other access model sought to treat advertising time as a nondiscriminatory public space. In this model, the media would have sold their designated advertising space to all responsible entities seeking to express their views. Content neutral and narrowly drawn, this policy would have required broadcasters to accept advertising on a nondiscriminatory basis and would have affected only a small portion of broadcasters' schedules. The various outcomes of these cases aside, both models of access were feasible under an empowering view of speech rights.

The Supreme Court's decisions in *Red Lion*, *CBS v. DNC*, and *Miami Herald* define the conditions under which ordinary citizens can participate in social mediation through print and broadcasting. Instead of enabling citizens to circulate information reflecting their diverse views and experiences, the Court treated the ability to send information and the ability to receive it as distinct and divisible aspects of speech rights. Nor did the Court give equal treatment to the public's speech rights within these media. The Court upheld the right to receive information in broadcast, but denied it in print. It denied the right to send information in both. Furthermore, close examination of these cases shows that public speech rights received protection where empowering regimes applied, but failed to receive any protection from the defensive approach.

The *Red Lion* Court adopted a largely empowering definition of speech rights. The Court affirmed the public's speech rights in broadcasting. It also recognized that government action could enhance, as well as inhibit, speech. The Court deemed the Fairness Doctrine permissible government regulation because it did not call for program censorship, prevent broadcasters from speaking, or mandate the expression of government viewpoints. Rather, the doctrine effectively served to protect public rights, create speaking opportunities, and promote the general public interest. At the same time, *Red Lion's* support for an empowering regime was somewhat ambiguous. The Court upheld fairness policies that involved a right to receive diverse information and a limited right of access to the media, but it did so on the basis of a right to receive only. The Court did not endorse an integrated view of speech rights necessary to fully protect social mediation. It refused to consider whether economic scarcity or the role of broadcasting in a democratic society warranted government protection of the public's speech rights, as a more thoroughly empowering approach would have done. Rather, the Court argued that government allocation of broadcast spectrum and public ownership of the airwaves gave the government discretion to decide whether the public would have limited speech rights in this medium.

In *CBS v. DNC,* the Court was asked to define the parameters and limits of the public's speech rights. The defendants in the case, as well as their supporters, argued that the public's speech rights include both a right to send and receive communication, that the public needs real spaces in which to actualize their rights, and that the government must affirmatively promote these conditions. The *CBS v. DNC* Court retreated from the empowering aspects of *Red Lion* and used a defensive approach to determine that the public's speech rights in broadcasting should be limited to a right to receive information. By solidifying the legal divide between the public's right to send and receive in broadcasting, the Court preserved *Red Lion's* affirmation of the public's speech rights without extending the public any right to speak. Concerned primarily with whether limited access policies violated the speech rights of broadcasters, the Court neglected to explore the implications of defining speech rights as a right to receive information only. In addition, the *CBS v. DNC* Court failed to make the critical distinction, recognized in *Red Lion,* between government actions that inhibit speech and those that create more speech. Given its defensive framework, the Court saw any right of access, however narrowly defined, as government usurpation of control over broadcast programming. In the logic of the Court, the broadcaster speaks for the public, while the public speaks only for private interests.

In *Miami Herald,* rather than protect speech rights, the First Amendment acts as a barrier to balanced political discussion and debate. The Court is so far steeped in the defensive tradition with respect to the print media that it cannot consider the potential benefits of a right of reply to the press. Nor can the speech interests of any group, other than the newspaper publisher, merit thoughtful examination. For the *Miami Herald* Court, all government action constitutes an abridgement of speech, and the government can never adequately justify the creation of speech opportunities for the public. Speech rights should follow the vicissitudes of the open market, regardless of the real opportunities provided therein.

The end result of the seminal cases examined here is that the public has highly qualified speech rights in the broadcast media and no speech rights in print. The Court tied the public's speech rights in broadcast to the public status of the airwaves and the necessity of government licensing. In rejecting speech rights in print, the Court was impervious to the actual conditions of print markets. Its inconsistency in assessing real conditions has meant less speech rights in print and more in broadcast, despite the facts that both media are equally inaccessible to most people and that most cities have more broadcasters than newspapers (Barron, *Public Rights* 177; Van Alstyne 86). Had the Court tied speech rights to the paucity of opportunities to participate in public debate or to the vital role that media play in democratic life, it could have avoided this contradiction.

Although the Court rejected media-access rights in print and broadcast, it left open the possibility of public access to multichannel media. In *CBS v. DNC* and *Miami Herald,* the Court cited what it considered to be the inevitable and objectionable consequences of media-access policies. As Tribe notes, the Court associated three potential harms with these policies (697). First, access policies triggered by media content may lead newspapers or broadcasters to censor themselves. Second, government-enforced access policies may result in the government manipulation of media content. Third, government regulation of access may tempt the government to exert other forms of control. Nevertheless, the Court held open the possibility that in the future the government might be able to devise access rules that steer clear of these perceived dangers. In fact, at the time that the Court decided *CBS v. DNC* and *Miami Herald,* such a policy was already taking shape. The rise of cable television, with its increased channel capacity, gave the FCC an opportunity to mandate the set-aside of entire channels for public access. The FCC envisioned these channels as public forums, or spaces that neither the government nor the cable operator could censor. Furthermore, the public's ability to speak over these channels would not be triggered by, or even linked to, the content of cable-operator speech. The constitutional status of public speech rights on these channels is the subject of the next chapter.

4   The Right to Public Space

DEMOCRATIC COMMUNICATION REQUIRES public spheres. In democratic societies, people need concrete sites where political discussion, debate, and deliberation take place. These are spaces where citizens can share their collective interests, engage in reasonable and responsible democratic decision-making, and send and receive communication that reflects their diverse experiences of the world. These are spaces of social mediation. In addition, their functionality depends on broad accessibility, universal inclusiveness, and relative freedom from economic or state control (Garnham, *Capitalism and Communication* 108–9; Habermas; Fraser 109). Open and accessible markets or other private spaces can be the setting of such democratic activities. But when markets fail to support these activities, governments must act to ensure their widespread availability through the creation and maintenance of public spaces in which the free-speech rights of the broader public are operative. The creation of public space is a prime means by which governments can maintain and protect democratic public spheres.

Given its importance to democratic processes, the legal status of public space is a central concern for democratic societies. Governments can create and secure democratic public spaces in the media only if the courts legitimize these spaces. Yet, the Supreme Court has never directly addressed the status of public space in print or broadcast. In these media, the Court has framed policies affecting speech primarily in terms of the right to send or receive communication, despite the fact that many of these policies also raise public-space concerns. For instance, policies that advocate media access or rights of reply presume that the government can sew pockets of public space into the garment of private media. Though the courts have ignored this question in print and broadcast, they have addressed questions of public space on cable television, primarily in relation to the legal status of public-access cable channels. In fact, the legal treatment of public-access channels is an important gauge of the legal standing of government-created public space in U.S. media law. Though often associated with low production values and unconventional content, these channels are archetypes of public communicative space. They are noncommercial, publicly available at little or no cost, and open to the public on a nondiscriminatory basis (Brenner and Price 6–38). By tradition, these channels operate as public forums, or spaces, where the public's right to speak is immune from government and private censorship (U.S. Congress: House, *Cable Franchise Policy* 30).

The Supreme Court addressed the constitutionality of public-access channels in *Denver Area Educational Telecommunications Consortium v. FCC.* The central question underlying the case was whether public-access channels are legitimate public forums where everyone has speech rights or private property illegitimately taken from cable operators who have exclusive speech rights over these channels. Rather than affirm the public's speech rights, the Court resolved the case without deciding the speech regime appropriate to these channels. Moreover, separate opinions written by members of the Court clashed over both the constitutional status of these channels and who exactly should have speech rights on them. The language and logic of these separate opinions throws into stark relief the ways in which defensive and empowering speech rights regimes differ in their views of the legitimacy of public space in the media. These separate opinions are important indicators of the future prospects of government-created public space in privately held media.

The constitutional status of public-access cable channels and the First Amendment debates that swirl around them are also important markers of democratic prospects in another respect. The treatment of public space on cable television may foreshadow the treatment of public space on other broadband media. Cable television was the first medium where a single operator or owner had multiple channels at their disposal. Cable's relative channel abundance, in comparison to single-channel media like print and broadcast, led policy-makers to contemplate reserving some channels on each system for speech by others. Broadband-cable systems allowed policy-makers to allocate whole channels to public expression on a content-neutral basis. That is, they could create spaces in which the public's right to speak was not triggered by, and was completely disassociated from, the cable operator's speech. The legal treatment of public space on cable television serves as a signpost for how law might treat such spaces in other broadband media, like multiplexed broadcast channels, satellite television, and computer networks, and whether policy-makers can even contemplate such spaces in the future.

In this chapter, I map the law and policy history of public-access television. Though public-access television emanated from an empowering view of speech rights, the Court has never fully validated this vision. Public-access television and its users lack a secure legal standing with respect to speech rights. Numerous lower court cases have challenged the continued viability of public-access television, as have both the Cable Television Consumer Protection and Competition Act of 1992 and the Telecommunications Act of 1996. These latter challenges culminated in the *Denver Area* case, which contemplated the status of public space on privately owned, broadband media. A close reading of *Denver Area* suggests that access television is a legally vulnerable public space that raises extremely difficult questions for a legal system striven by conflicting views of speech rights. I argue further that contemporary public-forum law, the most obvious candidate for protecting public space in the media, presently lacks the capacity to do so. Without firm First Amendment protections, the future of public space in U.S. media remains precarious.

The Evolution of Public-Access Television Policy

From its beginning, U.S. public-access television policy has been rooted in an empowering view of speech rights. The FCC began encouraging cable operators to provide public-access channels in 1969. Taking note of the growing number of channels on cable systems and the tendency of single cable operators to monopolize service in their areas, the FCC suggested that the larger operators should act as common carriers on some channels. Reserving limited channels for common carriage would ward off exclusive cable-operator control over programming and increase opportunities for local and community expression (U.S. FCC, "CATV First Report" 202, 205). In 1972, the FCC outlined a comprehensive plan for cable regulation and included public-access television as one of its policy goals. This marked a high point in the development of public-access television (Engelman). The agency required cable operators in the one hundred largest markets to reserve channels for PEG access (U.S. FCC, "Cable Television Report" 143, 197). These channels would be noncommercial and available on a first-come, first-served basis to the public (190). Cable operators would charge the public nothing to access these channels and provide production services and facilities at a low cost (196). In order to safeguard the public's speech rights, cable operators were to have no control over, or liability for, content on these channels. Individual programmers would be legally responsible for whatever they might choose to say (195–96). The FCC tinkered with these rules a few years later, scaling down some of its earlier expectations for cable operators.[1] Yet, it continued to promote public-access television as a means to augment outlets for local expression, encourage program diversity, foster openness and participation in video communication, facilitate democratic institutions and processes, and provide informational and educational resources (294).

Despite strong FCC support, the Supreme Court struck down the 1972 access rules in *FCC v. Midwest Video* (1979). Midwest Video Corporation, a cable multisystem operator, had objected to the rules. In their view, the rules violated the editorial prerogatives of cable operators, wrongly forced cable systems to offer common-carrier services, and overstepped the FCC's rulemaking authority. The FCC had replied that it could legitimately promulgate rules designed to nurture localism and diversity and to encourage the public exchange of ideas (*FCC v. Midwest Video* 694–95). Dodging the First Amendment questions involved, the Court decided that the FCC was not authorized to create a system of nondiscriminatory access to cable television. The Court reasoned that cable companies were analogous to broadcast stations. Since the 1934 Communications Act forbade the treatment of broadcasters as common carriers, this prohibition also applied to cable operators. Although the Court revoked the FCC access rules, it left open the possibility that Congress or individual cities could mandate access (*FCC v. Midwest Video* 710). In many places, public-access channels would continue by virtue of franchise agreements negotiated by city governments.

Five years later, Congress outlined its own policies on public-access television in the Cable Communications Policy Act of 1984. Congress expressed support for public-access channels, noting that they furthered the act's goal of providing "the widest possible diversity of information sources and services to the public" (2780). A House of Representatives report on the act said, "Public access channels are often the video equivalent of the speaker's soap box or the electronic parallel to the printed leaflet. They provide groups and individuals who generally have not had access to the electronic media with the opportunity to become sources of information in the electronic marketplace of ideas" (U.S. Congress: House, *Cable Franchise Policy* 30). The act codified some of the common practices and arrangements surrounding public-access television (Roberts 133) and preserved the ability of cities to require PEG-channel space, facilities, and equipment as part of their cable franchise. The act also prohibited cable operators from exercising any editorial control over PEG-channel content and immunized them from liability (Cable Communications Policy Act of 1984 2801).[2] Yet, while Congress had implied that public-access channels were effectively public forums, the act never formally acknowledged this point.

Lower courts have been divided on the constitutionality of public-access channels. Several courts have affirmed the government's authority to create these channels. In *Erie Telecommunications v. City of Erie* (1988) and *Berkshire Cablevision of Rhode Island v. Burke* (1985), federal appeals courts confirmed the legitimacy of PEG-access requirements. According to these courts, the access rules were content neutral and served a compelling government interest—the promotion of the First Amendment rights of cable viewers and the open flow of information. Even more dramatically, in *Missouri Knights of the Ku Klux Klan v. Kansas City* (1989), a federal district court declared public-access television a bona fide public forum. The court characterized these channels as government-controlled property dedicated to public expression and held that neither the government nor the cable operator could censor speech in these forums. However, other cases have dismissed the idea that the government has a legitimate and compelling interest in mandating public access to cable television, including *Century Federal v. City of Palo Alto* (1986) and *Quincy Cable TV v. FCC* (1985).

The Cable Television Consumer Protection and Competition Act of 1992 again altered the configuration of public-access television. In a bid to protect children from indecent program content, Congress required the FCC to develop regulations that would allow cable operators to prohibit PEG-access programs depicting obscene, sexually explicit, or unlawful conduct. This part of the act modified the earlier requirement that cable operators exercise no editorial control over program content and made cable operators liable for obscene and indecent programming on these channels (Cable Television Consumer Protection and Competition Act of 1992 sec. 10c). The Telecommunications Act of 1996 reiterated these provisions, asking the FCC to permit cable-operator censorship of public-access programs containing obscenity, indecency, and nudity.

By giving cable operators editorial control over, and liability for, program content, the 1992 and 1996 acts raised the question of exactly who controls these channels. Asking cable operators to police indecency, a category of speech not considered illegal, undermined the notion of public-access channels as public forums where the programmer's right to speak is primary. If cable operators are responsible for program content, then public-access channels are not public forums where access programmers have speech rights but private spaces where speech rights belong only to the cable operator. The 1992 and 1996 acts challenged, albeit indirectly, the idea of public-access channels as public spaces and threatened their continued viability. The potential seriousness of this challenge was underscored by a 1995 appeals court ruling that examined the constitutionality of the indecency rules. The court found the rules permissible. In *Alliance for Community Media v. FCC*, the court argued that public-access channels were not public forums and that programmers and viewers had no First Amendment rights there.[3]

Deciding Not to Decide: The Plurality Opinion *in* Denver Area

The Supreme Court reversed this ruling in *Denver Area*. Five of the nine members of the Court found cable-operator censorship of indecent public-access programs unconstitutional (*Denver Area* 729–31). Leased-access channels, also subject to the 1992 and 1996 indecency rules, did not fare so well.[4] According to the plurality opinion, the PEG indecency rules were not necessary to protect children, and cable operators' longstanding lack of control over these channels weakened their claims to speech rights there (761, 766). Although the decision protected public-access channels from censorship by cable operators, it did not confirm the empowering speech regime that animates these channels. Instead, the Court tried to balance the interests of different parties without affirming the legal status of access channels or the speech rights of their programmers. Without this affirmation, public-access channels continue to be vulnerable to First Amendment challenges (Hops 15, 21–22).

The *Denver Area* Court refused to categorize public-access channels as either public forums or private property. Worried that changes in technology and industry would inevitably transform the cable landscape, the Court eschewed these categorizations (740, 743). The plurality argued that their determination of speech rights did not depend on the legal status of public-access channels. In their thinking, "the interests of programmers, viewers, cable operators, and children are the same, whether we characterize Congress' decision as one that limits access to a public forum, discriminates in common carriage, or constrains speech because of its content" (750). Yet, this argument is both untenable and paradoxical. The Court refused to categorize PEG-access channels because to do so definitively frames the social interests at stake, while at the same time arguing that such frames do not define or determine social interests. In fact, attaching the label of public forum or private property to public-access channels makes a world of difference in terms of how courts understand speech rights in these spaces. First Amendment legal traditions dictate that the public has speech rights in public forums, while only property owners have speech rights on private property (*Hudgens v. NLRB* [1976]; *Lloyd v. Tanner* [1972]).

Rather than adopt a standard of review pertaining to private-property or public-forum law, the Court used an ad hoc balancing approach to resolve the conflict. According to the Court, two sets of interests were at stake—the government's interest in protecting children from indecency and the competing speech interests of cable operators and public-access programmers (*Denver Area* 743). Access rules serve programmers' interests by increasing opportunities for expression, but disserve cable operators by limiting their control over some cable channels (743–44). To decide the case, the plurality invented a new standard, called "close scrutiny," that asked whether the rules were "appropriately tailored" to address "an extremely important problem" without unduly restricting speech (743). In the Court's view, the PEG indecency rules failed this test. For one thing, indecent speech did not seem to be a problem on public-access channels, and the FCC had not produced any evidence to the contrary (764–65). In addition, even had indecency been a problem, less restrictive and more appropriately tailored means were available to redress it. Most cable franchise agreements created local channel managers and supervisory boards who set program policy and effectively regulated indecent programming (761–62). Moreover, local managers were less likely than cable operators to exclude or undervalue borderline programs that pushed the envelope of acceptability (763). Finally, the Court found that access programmers have special access rights created by cable franchise agreements. These rights weighed more heavily in the balance against cable operators' speech rights since operators traditionally had no editorial control over these channels (761). Rather than analyze the relevant constitutional issues involved, the Court simply presumed that cable operators had less of a speech interest over these channels because that had always been the case.

The plurality opinion in *Denver Area* used neither a defensive nor empowering approach to speech rights. The Court left the legal status of PEG-access channels and their users undecided, opting instead for an ad hoc balance of dimly defined interests. The Court concluded that the indecency rules were in violation of the First Amendment, but it did not clarify exactly whose rights were being violated and in what way. For example, the Court did not decide whether cable franchise agreements create a speech right for the local channel managers and supervisory boards who set policy on these channels. Nor did the Court offer an affirmative defense of access programmers' speech rights. In fact, the Court gave no compelling reason why access should be considered a right apart from history and custom (*Denver Area* 734, 761). The Court simply took a hands-off approach to existing arrangements. Consequently, it protected public space on privately owned media by default only. *Denver Area* offers public-access channels and users no protection against future First Amendment challenges, especially if those challenges result from rules and regulations better tailored to respond to more important problems.

Free Speech or Forced Speech? The Real Debate *in* Denver Area

The plurality did not articulate a First Amendment regime for public-access channels, but several Supreme Court justices addressed the subject in separate opinions. Two of these opinions, written by Justice Kennedy and Justice Thomas, contain detailed, though conflicting, analyses of speech rights on public-access channels. These separate opinions show two different ways that the Court is likely to interpret the legal status of PEG-access channels if and when it deals with this question directly. The Kennedy and Thomas opinions square off over whether cable access channels embody free or forced speech, and in so doing they illustrate the widely divergent interpretations of public communicative space proffered by empowering and defensive approaches to speech rights.

In a concurring opinion, Justice Kennedy (joined by Justice Ginsburg) called the indecency rules unconstitutional, but for reasons other than those expressed by the plurality (*Denver Area* 780–81). Drawing on an empowering approach to speech rights, Kennedy argued that public-access channels are public forums (783). When government opens up property to public expression, it creates a designated public forum in which the public at large has speech rights, not just a privilege to speak (*International Society for Krishna Consciousness v. Lee* [1972]). Neither the state nor the cable operator can censor speech on these channels (*Denver Area* 798–99). Moreover, legal precedent holds that public forums can extend beyond physical spaces, like streets and parks, and beyond government-owned property (792). In the case of public-access channels, local governments contract with cable operators to provide a public right of access to the cable system in exchange for cable-operator access to public rights-of-way (793–94). This contract is the genesis of access rights. Kennedy wrote, "A franchise agreement is a contract, and in those agreements the cable operator surrenders his power to exclude certain programmers from the use of his property for specific purposes. A state court confronted with the issue would likely hold the franchise agreement to create a right of access equivalent to an easement in land. So one can even view this case as a local government's dedication of its own property interest to speech by members of the public" (794). For Kennedy, public-access channels are a legitimate government undertaking comparable to the creation of a public easement on private property. The government can, when it sees the need, expand the public's speaking opportunities.

Kennedy explicitly categorizes public-access channels as public forums, thereby invoking a First Amendment regime that recognizes the speech rights of public-access channel users and calls for strict scrutiny of any content-based regulations of speech (*Denver Area* 805). Under the strict-scrutiny standard, content-based regulations must be narrowly tailored to meet a compelling government interest (805). For Kennedy, the plurality's invention of the "close scrutiny" standard, which asked that regulations be appropriately tailored to remedy an extremely important problem, unnecessarily disregarded a clear and appropriate standard of legal review (786).

Furthermore, the indecency rules could not survive the strict-scrutiny test. Though the government has a compelling interest in shielding children from indecent speech, it has no interest in giving cable operators editorial discretion over PEG-access channels (*Denver Area* 805). In addition, the rules were not narrowly tailored. Because they allowed cable operators to ban indecent programming at their discretion, the rules gave protection from indecency only at "the caprice of the cable operator" (807). Finally, Kennedy argued that the indecency rules improperly restricted public speech by giving cable operators "a power under federal law, defined by reference to the content of speech, to override the franchise agreement and undercut the public forum the agreement creates" (793). For Kennedy, the indecency rules clearly violated the speech rights of public-access programmers.

In his dissent to *Denver Area,* Justice Thomas (joined by Justices Rehnquist and Scalia) framed public-access channels through the lens of defensive speech rights. According to Thomas, the indecency rules were unconstitutional. All cable channels, including public-access channels, are private property over which only cable operators hold speech rights. They are not public forums because these exist only on government property (827). Therefore, the government has no legitimate interest in providing public access to cable. Thomas argued that broadcasting, with its unique problem of spectrum scarcity, was the only medium for which the Court had sanctioned a right of access. Since spectrum scarcity does not apply to cable systems, they should be subject to the same speech-rights regime governing print or utility companies. *Miami Herald* established that government regulations could not mandate a right of reply to the press or intrude on its editorial functions. *Pacific Gas & Electric v. Public Utilities Commission of California* held that utility companies could not be forced to include consumer messages in their billing envelopes. In Thomas's view, public-access channels constituted a similar transgression on cable-operator speech rights. The indecency rules merely restored cable operators' editorial discretion over their own channels, something the government had no right to limit in the first place.

Thomas contended that ad hoc balancing was the wrong way to settle the case (*Denver Area* 818). Since they had no property interests in cable, programmers and viewers had no speech rights to balance. Thomas said, "Because the access provisions are part of a scheme that restricts the free-speech rights of cable operators, and expands the speaking opportunities of access programmers, who have no underlying constitutional right to speak through the cable medium, I do not believe that access programmers can challenge the scheme, or a particular part of it, as an abridgment of their 'freedom of speech'" (823). Public-access channels infringe on the editorial rights of cable operators by allowing people to speak who have no right to do so. By making cable operators a conduit for free speech by the public, the government improperly forces them to carry the message of the access programmer. For Thomas, public-access channels represent forced, not free, speech.

Thomas premised his understanding of the indecency rules on his belief that public-access channels are themselves unconstitutional (*Denver Area* 820–21). He argued that public-access channel requirements are subject to intermediate scrutiny, a standard of review applied in *Turner Broadcasting System v. FCC* in 1994, which looked at the constitutionality of government regulations requiring cable operators to carry broadcast signals. Under intermediate scrutiny, content-neutral regulations can stand only if they support "important government interests unrelated to the suppression of free speech and are no greater than essential to further the asserted interest"

(*Denver Area* 821). Though he identifies that standard, Thomas never considers whether the government might have a significant interest in creating speaking opportunities for the public. He simply states that access is not a constitutional right and that there is no compelling reason to burden cable-operator speech with access regulations (821–22).[5] Thomas prefers to leave speech opportunities in cable to the competitive market.[6] Within his defensive framework, the notion that the government might have a genuine interest in maintaining public communicative spaces is altogether alien.

The Future of Public Space on Cable Television and Other Multichannel Media

A 1984 congressional report on cable legislation, anticipating possible objections to public-access television policy, addressed the fit between access rules and First Amendment goals (U.S. Congress: House, *Cable Franchise Policy* 31–36). The report stated that the government has a "significant and compelling" interest in promoting and protecting values associated with free speech (34). These values include creating local outlets for free expression, ensuring that sources other than media owners have access to electronic media, promoting diverse viewpoints and information services, and maintaining an open and vibrant marketplace of ideas (30–34). Congress thought that public-access television not only furthered these values, but that it did so in a way that did not infringe on the speech rights of cable operators (19). The report deemed public-access television a content-neutral, structural regulation, similar to antitrust and cross-ownership rules, which sought to protect diverse information sources (33).[7] Access rules could not "chill" cable-operator speech since they are not triggered by anything the operator actually says. In the case of public-access television, cable operators act as conduits for expression on a few channels, while continuing to have editorial discretion over the majority of their channels (35). In fact, the report characterized the access rules as "narrowly drawn structural regulations" that fulfill First Amendment goals without influencing the content of cable-operator expression (35).

By 1984, the Supreme Court had already thrown out models of access designed for single-channel media, like print and broadcast. In both *Miami Herald* and *CBS v. DNC*, the Court argued that even limited rights of access to single-channel media would chill media speech and bring about government control of media content. But in *CBS v. DNC*, the Court had intimated that a constitutionally workable access arrangement might be possible for cable television.[8] Public-access television represented a new strategy for media access. Rather than link access rules to media speech or to single channels, the new rules set aside a few channels on multichannel media for public expression. Ultimately, the Supreme Court must determine the constitutionality of this strategy. Since the Court has yet to decide the legal status of public-access television, however, it is useful to conjecture whether public-forum doctrine, as it now stands, can offer protection to these public spaces created by government fiat.

Public-access television is modeled after public forums. As presently understood by the courts, however, public-forum law offers little hope of First Amendment protections to public-access channels or their users. Public-forum law originated in 1939 with *Hague v. CIO*, a case that forbid the government from abridging speech in spaces traditionally open to the public.[9] *Hague* invented the concept of the "traditional" public forum and linked public-forum law to the use of public property (Post 1718–19). Subsequent cases declared that private property open to the public for commercial purposes did not qualify as a public forum (*Hudgens v. NLRB; Lloyd v. Tanner*). As it has evolved, public-forum law has come to rely on the categorization and labeling of the type of property involved to determine whether and to what extent public expression deserves protection (Post). Today, public-forum status usually hinges on whether the courts characterize a property as public or private and whether that property traditionally has hosted public expression.

Public-access television does not conform to the current legal understanding of public forums. First, public-access television is not public property, but privately held property that the government has dedicated to public expression by contract. Consequently, it lies outside even the standard definition of a designated public forum, which requires that the government reserve *public* property for expressive purposes.[10] Nor does public-access television fit within the purview of "traditional" public forums or spaces that the government has managed "immemorially" for public use. Although public-access channels have always operated as though they were public forums, cable television is a more or less new medium with a relatively brief history of public management. And as Thomas points out in his dissent, the Court has steadily refused to apply public-forum law to spaces, like bus and train stations, that historically have operated under private ownership (*Denver Area* 826–27). In light of this interpretive tradition, public-access television is not a likely candidate for traditional public-forum status. Nor for that matter is any other U.S. communications technology, since all are relatively new, and all are privately owned or operated.

Public-forum law will need substantial rethinking and revision before it can protect public space in U.S. media. Because it is based mainly on the public-private property distinction, contemporary public-forum law side-steps, rather than engages, substantive questions related to speech rights. As critics of public-forum law note, its heavy reliance on categories of property undervalues the meaning of "public" and leads to a convoluted system of rules built upon highly problematic distinctions (Post 1715). The reformation of public-forum law must begin by challenging the use of property distinctions to define speech rights, as well as the very idea that there is a sharp dividing line between public and private property. Only by recognizing the fallacy of this division can the courts clear the way for public-forum law to be decided on more germane criteria. These criteria include the public function of communicative spaces and the democratic and social values that these spaces serve.

Like its approach to speech rights, the neoliberal approach of property rights is defensive. Neoliberals view the phenomena of property and its ownership as naturally occurring. In their view, the protection of property rights requires an impermeable barrier between the domain of property owners and the actions of government. Critics of this view challenge these assumptions by pointing out that property and its protection are not facts of nature, but the creation of governments (Boyle 27, 49; Mensch 13, 23; Michelman 1319, 1335–36; Streeter 207–8). Property is not an inert category that can be neatly labeled public or private, but a social determination of rights and entitlements (Boyle 27; Streeter 207). The critics, including the Legal Realists and critical legal-studies scholars, view rights through the framework of partici-patory-democratic theory. In this framework, rights are socially constructed and cannot exist separate from society. In fact, government action is the very foundation of property rights since it is the government that grants property holders their legal powers over the resources they control. In this sense, property rights are government-conferred privileges that distribute resources and power and endorse certain values and social relationships. There can be no hard and fast dividing line between "private" property rights and government action. This holds true particularly for electronic media, which rely on government to maintain their structure, operation, and control (Streeter 324).

Given that government constructs property rights and that public-private distinctions are ambiguous at best, public-forum law would do better to decide speech rights on the basis of the social values privileged in a specific configuration of property rights, rather than upon formal categories of property. Nor is it appropriate to decide speech rights according to a property's traditional uses. Speech rights are grounded in social and moral claims to serve the common good, not in custom or tradition. The creation and maintenance of a public space for democratic discussion and debate is a core democratic value. As participatory-democratic theory argues, public spheres are essential to democratic processes of social mediation, and governments must be able to foster these spaces absent their spontaneous generation in everyday life and in the real conditions of the marketplace. And, certainly, the law should not preclude the ability of the government to create public space in order to bolster democratic communication. As I will argue in chapter six, an alternative view of public-forum law, capable of supporting democratic communication, dwells in early case law around public forums and in the dissents to its landmark cases.

Conclusion

Although public-access television has been around since the 1960s, its status as a public space remains uncertain. Neither Congress nor the Supreme Court has recognized public-access channels as legal public forums. Furthermore, the Court has not granted access users speech rights on these channels, and it has not endorsed the empowering speech regime epitomized by access-television policy and tradition. The Court has upheld access provisions without making clear their relationship to speech rights. Thus, though the *Denver Area* decision preserved public-access television, it provided no precedent to resolve future disputes over these channels (Greenhouse A1, A8; McConnell). Without congressional and judicial recognition, public-access television continues to be highly vulnerable to First Amendment challenges, and lawmakers and policy-makers place a valuable site for democratic communication in jeopardy.

More than just public-access channels are at stake, however. From a legal standpoint, public-access channels represent both a specific set of channels residing on local cable systems and a larger idea—the idea of public space on privately held multichannel media. While some may take issue with the quality of public-access programming and question how effectively it contributes to local and national debate, these channels nevertheless provide a forum for democratic communication. They are the home to programming, not found on commercial or public television, that gives people a chance to bear witness, vocalize dissent, articulate alternative viewpoints, and engage in the myriad forms of democratic talk described by Benjamin Barber (Stein, "Access Television," "Democratic 'Talk'"). Perhaps even more important, these channels are only one example of the types of democratic institutions that people can build in what the law determines to be legitimate public spaces. Better and more effective configurations might exist, but they can be realized only if the greater principle behind them stands. To strike down public-access television rules on constitutional grounds is to strike down the very idea of public space in most contemporary media. If public-access channels cannot survive on cable television, it is doubtful that other public spaces on other multichannel media could outlast such a damaging precedent.

The Supreme Court's reticence to give a First Amendment stamp of approval to access channels and their users reflects deep tensions in U.S. law over the legitimacy of public communicative space on privately owned media. The separate opinions in *Denver Area* plainly illustrate the available choices. The defensive approach to speech rights negates the value of public communicative space in democratic processes. In this view, speech rights belong exclusively to property owners, and the government cannot legitimately create public spaces on private property. Consequently, the defensive approach rules out public space on virtually all U.S. media. Empowering speech regimes, on the other hand, allow the government to establish public communicative spaces where they are needed and recognize these spaces as legitimate sites of democratic activity.

5   Democratic Speech Rights
        on the Internet

FUNDAMENTALLY, DEMOCRATIC COMMUNICATION requires the ability to send communication, to receive it, and to create public spaces for social mediation. These conditions are the foundation of democratic speech rights, or speech rights that serve democracies. Nevertheless, as we have discussed in the preceding chapters, First Amendment interpretations offer only limited protection to these vital components of democratic communication in the traditional mass media. In *Miami Herald,* the Supreme Court rebuffed the efforts of states to create a right of access to print media. At the same time, the Court only partially upheld the public's speech rights in broadcasting. While championing the public's right to receive broadcast information in *Red Lion,* the Court in *CBS v. DNC* denied the public the actual opportunity to speak in this medium. Nor has the Court been willing to grant constitutional protection to public space on cable television. Although cable-access channels have operated for decades as if empowering speech rights guide their use, *Denver Area* showed that speech in these forums has no real First Amendment aegis.

Will the Internet provide a forum for democratic communication when more established media have not? The Internet is a network of networks, owned and operated by a mixture of public and private entities that voluntarily share open-network protocols. It provides a relatively affordable, open, and equitable communications environment. Presently, people can access the Internet at little or no cost through a variety of organizations, ranging from commercial ISPs and private computer systems to libraries, nonprofit groups, and educational institutions.[1] With Internet access, the possibilities for democratic communication are many. People can send and receive communication without interference from centralized mediators and gatekeepers. Electronic mail (e-mail), bulletin boards, list services, web logs, real-time communication, and unmoderated newsgroups facilitate dialog and discussion around a broad array of topics. For much of its history, most Internet communication has traveled over universally accessible telephone lines that have been mandated by law to connect with ISPs on nondiscriminatory and reasonable terms (Cooper 1026). As a result, Internet users have had their choice among numerous ISPs who have competed on price, terms, and conditions of service.[2] Consumer choice among ISPs has made attempts to control content by individual ISPs less likely and less effective, since consumers could respond by switching to a new ISP (Newhagen and Rafaeli 13). To date, few ISPs have constrained or rationed network bandwidth, or the capacity available to their users, and few have differentiated or prioritized among users. Such egalitarian behavior, along with the common practice of processing network transactions on a first-come, first-served basis, has contributed to equality of service on the network (Shenker 318). These characteristics—affordability, openness, and equality—have made the Internet a potential forum for democratic communication.

Many commentators acknowledge the nexus between the Internet and democratic communication (Aurigi 60; Behlendorf 151; Cooper 1011; Downing 157; and Sassen 177). In popular discourse, moreover, the Internet seems poised to overcome the problems of older media that failed to serve democratic communication. Many characterize the Internet as an open medium and public space where Internet users enjoy seemingly limitless opportunities to create, collect, and circulate information. Whether we view the Internet as an ideal forum for democratic communication, the Internet does offer real opportunities for social mediation that transcend distance. Conditions online are such that the possibility of experimenting with different methods and modes of social mediation abound. If we want the Internet to serve the communicative needs of a democratic society, we need to maintain these conditions.

Unfortunately, the current conditions surrounding the Internet are not unchangeable. The Internet faces pressures to change, and as Lessig points out, there is no reason why tomorrow's Internet must resemble the Internet of today (*Future of Ideas* 167). Alterations to hardware and software can transform network design. In the United States, both government and private interests are exerting pressure to change the Internet. Throughout the 1990s U.S. regulators contemplated a range of laws and legislation designed to alter the network's physical and intellectual infrastructure and control its information flows (Benkler, "Net Regulation" 1204). A number of these laws, namely the Communications Decency Act (CDA), the Child Online Protection Act (COPA), and the Children's Internet Protection Act (CIPA), cast about for acceptable ways to protect children from indecent communication. Private-market actors, for their part, seek to modify network design to suit their business strategies and economic interests. Some companies have begun to assert proprietary rights over network elements, such as computer servers and transmission pipelines. By doing so, they aim to achieve greater control over content flows, over the allocation of network resources, and over the terms and conditions of interconnection between themselves and ISPs. Both government and private actors have incentives to alter the current structure of the network, and law can facilitate or prohibit proposed changes in network usage, practice, and architecture.

A key question, in light of current pressures, is whether speech rights will protect the conditions necessary for democratic communication online. Will speech rights act as an effective barrier to changes that threaten affordability, openness, and equality on the Internet? Will they provide a justification for affirmative policies that aim to strengthen democratic communication? And will they prevent the government from imposing regulations on the Internet, including those designed to enhance speech? Although today's Internet is rich in speaking opportunities, these are not the same as speech rights. Opportunities unsupported by law can evaporate as conditions change. Rights, on the other hand, involve legal entitlements to speak that necessitate the presence of conditions that facilitate speech. Social conflicts over Internet structure and usage raise questions about who has the right to speak in these spaces and under what terms and conditions. Judicial answers to these questions will shape the speech-rights regime surrounding the Internet. Without empowering speech rights, the ability of the vast majority of network users to participate in democratic communication over the Internet is highly vulnerable to changing network conditions. With empowering speech rights, network users can assert their rights to speak against policies and practices that substantially damage speaking opportunities.

In this chapter, I examine evolving understandings of speech rights on the Internet in U.S. law. As with other areas of communication law, Internet case law draws on liberal-democratic theories of speech rights to analyze social conflicts over new technology. In so doing, the courts build an interpretive framework that determines the status of speech rights in new media. This framework can either help or harm the communicative goals of democratic societies. Talking about speech rights on the Internet is a somewhat speculative endeavor since U.S. law has yet to establish a definitive speech-rights regime for this new medium. Nevertheless, a number of court cases and several notable areas of legal conflict indicate how speech rights on this medium are likely to unfold. These areas of conflict center on government and private-sector attempts to censor potentially objectionable content and to change or control network infrastructure. Legal developments in these areas suggest that if a defensive speech regime prevails, law will effectively constrict the speech rights of Internet users in favor of the ability of ISPs and infrastructure owners or managers to monopolize speech. Furthermore, as one Supreme Court case suggests, the defensive approach may also fail to protect the public's speech rights from government censorship in public space. Since both government and private parties can act in ways that di-minish free speech, the law must adopt an empowering approach to speech rights, grounded in participatory-democratic theory, in order to preserve opportunities for democratic communication on the Internet.

The Internet, Democratic Communication, and Government Action

Many law and policy analysts deny that government has a positive role to play in securing freedom of speech on computer networks. An early pro-ponent of this view was Ithiel de Sola Pool. He argued that government regulation tends to stunt the development of new communication tech-nologies (*Technologies of Freedom*). According to Pool, computer network technology naturally favors decentralization, low costs, and ease of access.[3] If liberated from government regulation and left to a competitive market, the technology would provide a plurality of expressive outlets and ample opportunities for free speech. Along similar lines, others argue that net-work conditions, including openness, accessibility, the existence of multiple ISPs, and the capacity to transmit vast amounts of information, will protect free speech absent government regulation (Cate 43; Labunski 191–92). Such thinking invokes a defensive conception of speech rights. In this view, past and future Internet growth, as well as any social benefits emanating from the Internet, depends on the promotion of regulatory restraint and market competition.[4] From this neoliberal perspective, freedom equates with the outcomes of competitive markets, and the principal role of government is to facilitate these markets.

Others argue that securing democratic communication online calls for a more affirmative role for government. Skeptical of the ability of markets to adequately satisfy all social goals, these analysts maintain that democratic communication will thrive on the Internet only if the government protects these spaces from negative or harmful commercial forces (Lessig, *Code* 59; Lipschultz 3; McChesney 99; and Schiller 86). In this view, government must ensure that the media serve the needs of democratic society, including free-speech goals. A social commitment to democratic communication can and should translate into policies that protect and promote diverse content and sources, the ability of end users to both produce and consume information, open standards and infrastructures, universal access, and public space (Benkler, "Property" 7; Feld 23, 34; and McChesney 106, 118). Those who hold this perspective are cognizant of the many ways in which public funding and public regulation have contributed to the Internet's open structure. The Internet began as a government-sponsored research project. Federal policy ensured universal access to the telephone network on which the Internet was built. Federal mandates required nondiscriminatory interconnection between ISPs and the basic network infrastructure. The openness of computer networks has been not merely a result of technology, but also one of policy. In this view, free speech cannot be made subservient to either the government or the market. Nevertheless, the government, as an agent of the public, must act to protect democratic communication.

The claim that the Internet will inevitably serve as a forum for democratic communication if freed from government interference ignores the role of law and policy in creating and maintaining media systems in a democracy. The protection of democratic communication on new technologies requires not government inaction, but a government willing to take affirmative policy decisions that establish an environment hospitable to free speech without restricting or censoring speech. As with other media, how courts understand and interpret speech rights on the Internet will set the basic parameters for democratic communication in these spaces. The Internet speech-rights regime will determine what kinds of policies are acceptable or unacceptable, including those affecting who can speak, access information, control resources, and manage information flows. Legal conflicts around the right to send and receive information and the public or private status of Internet space implicate the key criteria of democratic communication. An evaluation of these conflicts, and how the courts apply law to them, suggests that whether the courts adopt an empowering or defensive approach may be a crucial factor in determining whether the Internet retains its democratic character.

The Right to Send and Receive Internet Communication

The right to send and receive communication on the Internet has been the focus of two Supreme Court cases involving the availability of indecent speech online. Although indecent speech receives some protection under First Amendment law, the government can make laws that restrict its time, place, and manner of presentation. Since 1996, Congress has made repeated attempts to shelter children from indecent communication online. The CDA, COPA, and CIPA all aimed to protect children from harmful speech on computer networks. Each of these laws sought to censor, rather than add, speech, and each has faced legal challenges.[5]

Indecency regulations are a political response to the fact that the Internet upsets societal norms surrounding indecency, pornography, and children. Computer networks are not subject to the same laws and norms that routinely shield children from sexually explicit materials in real space. For example, in real space children cannot enter adult-only stores, zoning laws prevent these stores from locating in areas where children routinely congregate, and discerning store clerks are unlikely to sell pornography to children. These safeguards do not currently exist in cyberspace. Whether deliberately or inadvertently, children can gain access to sexually explicit content and sites, and the producers and distributors of this material cannot always tell whether those seeking access are children or adults. As Benkler notes, the lack of intermediaries, organizational control points, and systems for discerning content or for granting social consent have destabilized controls on the flow of information ("Net Regulation" 1240). Indecency regulation is an attempt to extend social and cultural norms and standards to the Internet and to reestablish social controls destabilized by new technology (Rogerson and Thomas; Stein and Sinha; Wheeler).

In 1997, the Supreme Court decided its first case on Internet speech rights and indecency. The case, *Janet Reno v. American Civil Liberties Union,* centered on the constitutionality of two provisions in the CDA that criminalized the transmission and display of "indecent" and "patently offensive" speech to minors over computer networks. The act exempted from liability those who required proof of age or took "good faith, reasonable, effective, and appropriate actions" to ensure that no one under the age of eighteen could access content deemed harmful to minors (*Janet Reno v. ACLU* 844). The CDA immediately became a battleground between the free-speech interests of electronic publishers and the interests of government in seeking to shield children from harmful speech. Objecting to the act's provisions were ISPs, professional publishing associations, and organizations promoting civil rights, AIDS activism, and reproductive rights and services. These groups argued that the rules imposed substantial burdens on speech. The act would force speakers to take costly measures to screen users and to censor their own constitutionally protected speech. In its defense, the government maintained that it had the authority to impose time, place, and manner restrictions on indecent Internet speech. The government cited *FCC v. Pacifica,* a case sanctioning government regulation of indecent speech in broadcasting, and *Renton v. Playtime Theatres,* a case upholding zoning laws that banned adult theaters in residential neighborhoods, to support its position.[6]

To decide *Janet Reno v. ACLU,* the Supreme Court had to contemplate a speech regime for this new communications medium. The Court rejected the implicit analogy of the Internet to broadcasting suggested by the invocation of *FCC v. Pacifica.* It argued that *FCC v. Pacifica* did not apply because, unlike broadcasting, the Internet is not characterized by a history of extensive government regulation, frequency scarcity, or an invasive nature. The Court also rejected the zoning analogy in *Renton,* saying that the CDA rules were not time, place, and manner restrictions, but explicit regulations on the content of speech (*Janet Reno v. ACLU* 868). Instead, the Court saw the Internet as a "wholly new medium for worldwide communication" (850). In this democratic setting, communication resources are abundant, anyone with access to the Internet is a potential publisher, people can disseminate information free from constraints imposed by centralized gatekeepers, and communication is as diverse as human thought (870). Government regulation of Internet speech would have to withstand a strict-scrutiny test. That is, the government would have to show that the challenged sections of the CDA were narrowly tailored to serve a compelling government interest without unduly burdening speech.

In the Court's opinion, the CDA provisions failed the test. While it did not dispute the government's interest in protecting minors from indecent speech, the Court thought that the rules were poorly tailored to meet government aims and constituted a substantial burden on speech. The rules were vague and overbroad. Ambiguity over the exact meaning of the terms "indecent" and "patently offensive" would permit arbitrary enforcement of the rules and chill speech around controversial topics, like birth control and homosexuality. Because of their overbreadth, the rules were likely to suppress constitutionally protected speech and limit the level of discourse available to adults to that which was suitable for children (*Bolger v. Youngs*

Drug Products, cited in *Janet Reno v. ACLU* 875). In addition, the indemnity provisions in the act were infeasible. Without a standardized system for identifying indecent speech, potentially liable parties could never be sure that any precautions they took would be "effective." Finally, the costs associated with implementing and maintaining age-verification technology would place significant burdens on noncommercial and nonprofit speakers, potentially silencing these important sources of Internet speech. These costs were particularly unnecessary, said the Court, since user-based software provided a reasonable and effective means of shielding children from objectionable material.

The *Janet Reno v. ACLU* decision displayed an uneasy mix of defensive and empowering reasoning, ultimately taking a position that both participatory- and neoliberal-democratic theorists could endorse. All members of the Court, even those who are typically averse to government regulation, agreed that the government has an interest in protecting children from harmful speech (875). Consequently, all members of the Court in *Janet Reno v. ACLU* endorsed the empowering notion that the government can enact regulation in order to achieve a larger social good. In this case, that good was defined as maintaining cultural norms and standards of decency for children.

Although the Court accepted the validity of government regulation designed to protect children from indecency, it nevertheless struck down the CDA provisions because they were overly broad and would have corrupted a relatively hospitable environment for free speech. In making this determination, the Court took an empowering tack and looked at the real conditions that characterized Internet communication in 1996. The Court depicted the Internet as a robust forum for democratic communication. This new and unique medium, said the Court, offered anyone a "vast platform" to publish and distribute information at low cost and unimpeded by centralized gatekeepers (*Janet Reno v. ACLU* 853, 867). Recalling romantic images of free speech in early America, the Court noted that anyone with a phone line could become a virtual soapbox orator or pamphleteer on the Internet (870). According to the Court, this diverse democratic forum deserved full First Amendment protection (868–69). The government could best protect speech rights in this case by refraining from altering the conditions so conducive to free speech.

Despite these empowering elements, the majority opinion sounds a defensive note in its concluding paragraph when it states the Court's presumption that "government regulation of the content of speech is more likely to interfere with the free exchange of ideas than to encourage it" (*Janet Reno v.*

ACLU 885). And the decision to prevent government action in order to protect free speech sits comfortably with the defensive tradition. In many ways, the *Janet Reno v. ACLU* decision was equally acceptable to those who ascribe to a defensive or empowering view of speech rights. The Court protected the free-speech opportunities of communication senders, the targets of the CDA, by preventing government action. Since the CDA had sought to restrict the range of speech available, not to create additional speaking opportunities, the case did not raise questions of affirmative access that typically place the defensive and empowering traditions at odds. The government's role in structuring a more vibrant free-speech environment online was not at issue. And because the CDA provisions applied only to producers of information, the affirmative speech rights of ordinary Internet users were not at issue. Although the decision proclaimed full First Amendment protection for the medium, it did not specify exactly who has speech rights on the Internet and why. Ultimately, *Janet Reno v. ACLU* protected democratic communication simply by preventing government interference with the medium.

In another attempt to protect minors from objectionable material, Congress enacted the Children's Internet Protection Act. CIPA denies federal funding and Internet technology subsidies to libraries and schools that refuse to install filtering software on their computers. This software is intended to block content considered obscene, pornographic, or harmful to minors. The CDA and CIPA represent different strategies for controlling access to objectionable content on the Internet. The CDA tried to zone speech by placing certain sites and materials off limits to children. It assigned the burden and liability for protecting children to content producers and suppliers. Anyone who provided indecent materials would have had to develop procedures denying access to minors or risk criminal prosecution. CIPA approaches the problem of children's access to indecent material from another angle. It places strong incentives on public libraries and schools to act as content gatekeepers. By threatening to withhold financial resources, CIPA encourages, but does not directly force, schools and libraries to comply with the act. Schools and libraries that do not want to filter Internet access can choose to forego certain specified federal funds. Under CIPA, the burden is on the gatekeepers to install software programs that identify and block indecent content, and the government can maintain that libraries and schools voluntarily undertake this burden. Libraries, library patrons, web publishers, and others challenged the constitutionality of this law as it applied to libraries. The libraries argued that CIPA would impinge on their First Amendment right to offer the public constitutionally protected materials, since imprecise filtering software would inevitably block more material than necessary (*US v. American Library Association* 235).

The central issue in the case, according to the Court, was whether CIPA would force libraries to violate the speech rights of their users to access information over the Internet. The plurality on the Supreme Court held that it did not. Although a plurality opinion is not binding precedent with respect to points of law, the Court's reasoning in this case reveals the propensity of a defensive approach to undervalue speech rights in public spaces. The Court's reasoning hinged on two related points. Internet access through public libraries does not constitute a public space, and, consequently, the public has no speech rights in this setting. Invoking public-forum law, the Court found that the societal role of libraries is incompatible with the treatment of library Internet access as a public space in which library patrons had speech rights. Libraries exist to provide requisite and appropriate materials for their patrons, said the Court, and therefore must make selection decisions about the materials they acquire (*US v. ALA* 231, 233). Public-forum status would subject the library's collection decisions to strict scrutiny under the law and make it impossible for them to carry out their central function as arbiters of culture. Far from *Janet Reno v. ACLU's* characterization of the Internet as a speaker's corner and free-speech soapbox, the *US v. ALA* opinion described the Internet when accessed through public libraries as a mere conduit for the transmission of library approved materials, akin to a "technological extension of the book stack" (233). Since library patrons have no First Amendment right to receive or access information in these spaces, CIPA does not force libraries to violate the speech rights of library Internet users. In addition, the Court noted that the government can condition the receipt of federal monies on its own objectives—the objective in this case being to help libraries obtain suitable and appropriate materials without exposing children to harmful speech (231, 236–37). It also noted that the CIPA provision allowing libraries to disable filters at the user's request prevents the law from overblocking constitutionally protected speech, a feature that presumably keeps the law narrowly tailored (234).

The plurality opinion in *US v. ALA* utilizes a defensive framework that does not recognize the value of public spaces or of speech rights therein. Moreover, in this case, the defensive devaluing of public space and public rights (that is, rights for those other than the owners or managers of private property) overshadows the defensive principle of government inaction. Rather than declare a right to receive information that is already available in the decidedly public venue of the public library, the Court found that the government could control or manage these spaces in which the public has no rights. It is relevant to note that the Court could have upheld CIPA simply by declaring that it was sufficiently tailored to achieve a compelling government interest. Indeed, the Court did say that CIPA's disabling provision allowed it to overcome any constitutional objections to the law. However, the Court went further, treating public libraries as nonpublic forums in which library patrons had no speech rights. A nonpublic forum is a government-owned public space where free expression is sometimes allowed but where the recognition of public speech rights would conflict with the dedicated purpose of that property (*Greer v. Spock* 838). The Court viewed, although it did not label it as such, public library Internet access as a nonpublic forum whose function is to provide culturally appropriate materials, not to facilitate the free exchange of information and ideas. Because public space, public rights, and the process of social mediation count for so little from this perspective, the defensively minded Court was able to sanction restrictive government regulation of speech in these spaces.

While the plurality in *US v. ALA* was persuaded that library patrons have no right of access to information online, Justices Souter and Ginsburg disagreed.[7] In his dissent, Souter starts from the presumption that library Internet access is a public space in which the speech rights of library patrons are paramount. Public libraries are government agents that provide Internet access for public use. As such, libraries cannot interfere with patrons' First Amendment right to access lawful speech over the Internet without a narrowly tailored and compelling reason. According to Souter, CIPA fails this test. Although the government has a compelling interest in protecting children from indecency, contemporary filtering software is too faulty and crude, often blocking far more than indecent communication, and the wording of CIPA's disabling provision too uncertain, stating that libraries "may" unblock the filters but not requiring that they do, to protect speech that adults have the right to receive (*US v. ALA* 250). Nor does the societal role of libraries or the necessity of making collection decisions conflict with the speech rights of library patrons. According to Souter, the chief role of libraries is to provide broad access to information and ideas, not to judge what materials are suitable for the public. And once a library acquires Internet access, the decision to block some material becomes more akin to censorship than to a simple collection decision. Mandated blocking of Internet content violates the common library practice of making all of its holdings available to all adults and forces libraries to violate the First Amendment rights of library users (*US v. ALA* 253).

Souter's empowering perspective is better able to curtail government action that contracts, rather than expands, speech rights in public space. Souter presumes that the public does have speech rights in public libraries. Because he views library Internet access as an important space for receiving communication, as well as the free speech of patrons, he is willing to compromise the public's right to receive only if the strict-scrutiny test is met. In his analysis it is not, owing to defects in filtering software and the law itself. In addition, while Souter agrees that indecency regulation is a legitimate area of government regulation when narrowly tailored to serve a compelling interest, he makes an important distinction about the legitimacy of government regulation that the defensively minded plurality does not. He distinguishes between the library's role in making collection decisions and its ability to block content once acquired. While the former is a legitimate library function, the latter is not. Rather, it is like "buying a book and then keeping it from adults lacking an acceptable 'purpose,'" or "buying an encyclopedia and then cutting out pages with anything thought to be unsuitable for all adults" (*US v. ALA* 252). Schauer describes this distinction as the difference between a necessary and unnecessary choice situation (*Free Speech* 117–18). Necessary choices are made in the context of scarce acquisition resources and do not raise First Amendment concerns. Unnecessary choices are made when resources are abundant or no choice is required and clearly raise free-speech problems. While Souter's empowering position would allow government intervention in some circumstances, he rejects intervention in this case in part because of the distinction between necessary and unnecessary choice situations.

In the CIPA case, the defensive view of speech rights allowed government regulation, where the empowering view would not have. Why is it that the neoliberal perspective, which is almost synonymous with government inaction, failed to protect against government intervention in this case? And why did the participatory-democratic perspective, whose detractors frequently accuse it of treading the slippery slope of increased government intervention, argue against government censorship of Internet communication in public libraries? To answer these questions, we need to review the views that each of these theories holds on government action and the democratic value of public and private space. While the neoliberal approach to speech rights is commonly thought to prohibit all manner of government action and the participatory-democratic approach to allow it, this characterization is misleading and inaccurate. In reality, both approaches allow the government to structure communication resources. As I have noted earlier, neoliberalism looks to the government to structure the fundamental rules of the marketplace, including the media market. It is only once these rules are in place that further government intervention is discouraged. Legal protections for private space, private property, and the individual's right to manage or control these spaces are of prime concern within this theory. A main difference between neoliberal and participatory-democratic perspectives, then, is not that one allows government intervention while the other does not. Rather, the defensive approach is concerned almost exclusively with preventing unnecessary government intervention in the private sphere of the economy, seen as the locus of all rights, and therefore has little interest in the development of public spaces with public rights. In contrast, participatory-democratic theory recognizes the ability of government to structure space, whether public or private, so that the majority of citizens can find opportunities to exercise their rights. Moreover, while participatory-democratic theory recognizes the need for government action to create and maintain opportunities for free speech, it is nevertheless cognizant of the coercive power of government and the need to prevent the state from abridging speech rights within spaces of all types. As many free-speech theorists within the empowering tradition argue, the government can act affirmatively to protect the conditions necessary to free speech, but it cannot restrict or censor speech (Barron, "Access to the Press" 1676; Emerson, *System;* Sunstein). While this tradition favors government regulation that expands speech opportunities, it does not condone laws that censor speech and effectively strip people of their speech rights.

The CIPA case suggests that neoliberalism's exclusive focus on protecting private spheres of activity and its devaluing of public rights and spaces make it a poor candidate to protect public speech rights in public spaces. Because participatory-democratic theory focuses on the need for public rights and spaces in a democracy, this theory more strongly resists government actions that curb public rights in public spaces. It recognizes public space where neoliberalism, which lacks a strong conception of public space, does not. Thus, an empowering approach to speech rights is better equipped to protect the public's rights from government intervention in public spheres and spaces.

The CDA and CIPA resulted in cases that raise important questions about speech rights online, though they leave unanswered many questions about the exact configuration of Internet speech rights. Foremost among these questions are the following: Who has the affirmative right to speak in cyberspace—end users, ISPs, system operators, or infrastructure owners? To what extent are online spaces public or private? And what is the role, if any, of government in fostering democratic communication in these forums? In the remainder of this chapter, I look at how other areas of Internet law have begun to answer these questions that define the contours of Internet speech rights.

Who Can Speak on the Internet?

At present, the Internet gives its users the ability to speak through a variety of forums. Numerous and highly competitive ISPs offer access to the network, increasing the likelihood that end users can obtain access under favorable terms and conditions.[8] These ISPs provide Internet access through a variety of technical platforms, including the phone system, wireless technologies, and cable television systems. The existence of multiple ISPs, coupled with the open and nondiscriminatory hardware and software that has dominated the core telephone network over which much network communication travels, has meant that avenues of access and opportunities to speak abound. So much so that, in its current configuration, the Internet resembles a public communicative space. Library Internet access aside, social mediation takes place relatively free from centralized institutions, professional mediators, government censorship, and commercial pressures. Both the structure of the technology, shaped in part by the government mandate that phone networks act as common carriers, and the market have supported democratic communication on the Internet.

For other than library patrons, the Supreme Court has yet to make law on who has affirmative speech rights online or to delineate the respective speech rights of different categories of Internet speakers. To date, cases have not arisen that force the Court to decide these questions. Nevertheless, questions such as who are the real speakers on the Internet and what speech rights do they have there continue to surface. As the Internet grows and develops, many network actors, including infrastructure owners, ISPs, and end users, are putting forward free-speech claims. Conflict and uncertainty about the right to speak on the Internet cluster around disputes over who has the right to disseminate information and communication and who controls the network infrastructure. An examination of these areas of law reveals what is at stake regarding future determinations of speech rights for different network participants and for the structure of the Internet as a whole.

E-mail and the Right to Speak

The courts have examined the right to send communication in a handful of legal disputes over e-mail. E-mail programs allow the transmission of messages online. End users send e-mail messages from one address to another, where they are stored and processed on local computer servers before reaching their final destination. E-mail is analogous to the everyday mail that travels over the postal system. Unlike the public mail system, however, some of the servers and networks over which e-mail travels are private. Recall that the Internet is made up of many interconnected networks, both public and private, that voluntarily use open protocols in order to "talk" to one another. Private networks lease lines from the local telephone companies or establish their own wireless systems in order to serve a closed membership, as well as specific organizations or activities (Morley and Gelber 74–75). In several instances, owners of private networks and servers have sought to block unwanted e-mail from their systems. In one set of cases, commercial ISPs like AOL and CompuServe have blocked online junk mail from getting through to their system members. In another case, a computer-chip maker, Intel, has moved to block messages critical of the company from reaching its employees. These cases ask the courts to define the speech rights of end users against those of local private networks and ISPs. Legal developments in this area are contradictory but reveal the distinct possibility that speech rights could be thought of as rights that adhere to the owners of network hardware, software, and servers, rather than to end users.

One type of end user to test its right to send communication over the Internet is the commercial spammer. Spammers use e-mail to send unsolicited advertisements to Internet users. In the mid-1990s, AOL, CompuServe, and other ISPs took steps to stop commercial spam from reaching their subscribers. The ISPs argued that these unwanted messages burdened their servers and damaged their reputation. They also maintained that unsolicited commercial spam trespassed on their private servers and networks. In *Cyber Promotions v. America Online* (1996), advertising agency Cyber Promotions tried to defend its spamming practices by arguing that the Internet was a public system with a public function over which it had the right to send communication (*Cyber* 450). A Pennsylvania district court disagreed. In its view, private parties had no First Amendment right to send unsolicited e-mail advertisements over the Internet, and AOL could control its own network pathways in order to protect its private property and reputation (455). Although AOL provides its members with e-mail addresses so that they can communicate on the Internet, AOL's servers are not public spaces where anyone has a right to speak. In *CompuServe v. Cyber Promotions* (1997), an Ohio district court came to a similar conclusion. In this case, the court held that Cyber had no right to speak on CompuServe's private property. Although CompuServe gave customers e-mail addresses in order to communicate with other Internet users, CompuServe was a private actor whose computer equipment remained proprietary. CompuServe could restrict access to its system as it chose (*CompuServe* 1024). Cyber did not have a First Amendment right to send messages to unwilling recipients—the recipient in this case being CompuServe, said the court, not CompuServe's customers (1027). In both of these cases, the ability of commercial speakers to send communication ended at the proprietary servers of ISPs.

The above cases deal with commercial spam—a class of speech for which many have little sympathy. Noncommercial speech that does not significantly burden proprietary computer equipment may fare better with respect to speech rights. Consider the debate in the California courts over whether a private company can prevent persons from communicating with its employees. Although California trial and appeal courts followed the logic of the earlier spam-related cases, the California Supreme Court provided another way of looking at the right to send communication online. In the case of *Intel v. Hamidi* in 2003, the California Supreme Court overturned, though not without significant dissent, earlier rulings that had enjoined a former worker from sending e-mail to Intel employees. The conflict began when, after being dismissed by Intel, Ken Hamidi set up FACE-INTEL, an organization that offered Intel employees worldwide a forum to discuss employment conditions and other concerns related to the company. Over a two-year period, Hamidi sent six mass e-mailings to Intel employees over Intel's e-mail system. Intel asked the court to enjoin Hamidi from sending any more messages to e-mail addresses on its system, arguing that Hamidi's actions constituted a trespass to chattels. A somewhat archaic legal principle, this common-law tort occurs when someone uses or meddles with another's possessions. The California court of appeals earlier had held that a trespass to chattels occurred when Hamidi's electronic messages intruded on Intel's property and disrupted its community, even though his missives caused no measurable harm (*Intel* 248–49). The California Supreme Court reversed this decision, holding that contemporary California trespass to chattels law does not and should not cover occasional electronic communications that neither harm nor impair a company's use of its computers (36).[9] Unlike the high volume of messages sent from commercial spammers, Hamidi's infrequent messages did not significantly burden Intel's computers. In addition, the Court was reluctant to expand the tort to encompass property rights similar to those protecting land and its inviolability.[10] If every owner of network servers could exclude particular sources and messages at will, the openness and social benefits of Internet communication could be lost (49–50). Although the court did not specifically endorse Hamidi's right to speak online, it nevertheless refused to censor his speech without significant evidence that it harmed Intel's property. Several justices dissented from this position, arguing that only owners have speech rights on private property and that Intel's property rights allow it to determine who can send messages over its servers (74).

The *Intel* majority and dissenters also differed over who counts as the recipient of the e-mail messages and how to understand Internet space. The majority dismissed Intel's argument that it had a "right not to listen" to Hamidi's messages and thus not to receive them. The Court noted that, as the actual recipients of the messages only Intel's employees, not Intel, could claim a right not to listen (51). In contrast, because Intel owned and maintained the e-mail system that received the messages, the dissenters saw Intel as the real recipient of Hamidi's messages (54). In addition, the majority did not distinguish between public and private space on the network. It noted that Intel deliberately connected its e-mail system to the Internet and therefore knew that employees were likely to receive some unapproved communication (46–47). The openness of the network is part of what makes it valuable to users, including Intel and its employees, said the Court majority (49). Dissenters, on the other hand, stressed that Intel's computers are private property, not public forums for the speech of others (52, 67). One dissenter stated that "the majority fail to distinguish open communication in the public 'commons' of the Internet from unauthorized intermeddling on a private, proprietary intranet" (67). In the judge's view, the court could solve such conflicts by clearly delineating public from private networks. An outsider's right to communicate stops at the private servers that link to the Internet.

In many ways, the *Intel* case is a notable exception to evolving understandings of who has speech rights on the Internet. The court upheld the rights of end users, whether speakers or receivers, in part because the decision to connect to the Internet involves knowledge that one is entering a relatively open space that is not, and should not be, completely controllable. Although the court could have asserted the free-speech principles behind its decision more explicitly, it did offer a vision of the Internet as a quasipublic space in which private-property owners cannot simply set the terms and conditions of communication, a viewpoint resonant with an empowering approach to speech rights. The cases dealing with spam, and the dissents in *Intel,* offer a different vision of speech rights online. In this defensive vision, ordinary Internet end users have no right to speak. ISPs have exclusive, proprietary interests in their equipment and can therefore act as system gatekeepers. They can block unwanted e-mail and ban disfavored speakers. In this vision, the speech rights of ISPs stand in sharp contrast to those of common carriers who have no control over speech on their systems. Moreover, as all of the above cases show, ISPs may be motivated to act as gatekeepers for private reasons, even without government prompts such as indecency legislation. While law in this area remains underdeveloped, the above cases suggest that determinations of the right to speak online depend on whether online space is understood as public, quasipublic, or private and whether speaker status accords to end users or to the private ISPs who own and manage the network.

Infrastructure Owners and the Right to Speak: Broadband Networks, the Access Debate, and the *Brand X* Decision

The speech rights of those who own the physical pipelines over which communication travels were not in question until the late 1990s with the diffusion of broadband Internet services. Unlike the limited capacity of the narrowband telephone lines that originally served as the foundation of commercial Internet access, broadband networks have the capacity, or bandwidth, to send and receive large amounts of data at comparatively high speeds (U.S. FCC, "Deployment of Advanced Telecommunications" 2850; Morley and Gelber 7).[11] Broadband networks enable Internet content producers and end users to utilize advanced applications, substantially enhancing the online experience. With broadband, users can watch full-motion video, speedily upload and download movies and music, engage in Internet-based telephony or teleconferencing, flip through web pages as quickly as though they were the pages of a book, and make use of other bandwidth-intensive multimedia applications. Increasingly, the ability to utilize the new developments in Internet technologies, services, and applications depends on access to broadband services. Consequently, people are subscribing to high-speed Internet services in increasing numbers. In 2005, 55 percent of adult Internet users had broadband connections at home or at work, and in 2004 forty-eight million people had broadband at home, a 60 percent increase over the previous year (U.S. FCC, "Availability of Advanced Telecommunications" 20571). A variety of technological platforms can serve as a foundation for broadband services, including telephone, cable, terrestrial wireless, and satellite technologies. However, upgrading to broadband capacity requires enhancing current networks through digital-compression technology or deploying new technology, like fiber-optic cables, especially in the last mile to the home, where narrowband technology typically constrains network bandwidth.

Prior to the advent of broadband services, regulation of the Internet infrastructure closely paralleled that of telephone regulation. Early commercial Internet access, also known as "dial-up," used the preexisting open and ubiquitous "narrowband" telephone network to transport its messages. Long regulated as a common carrier in which the infrastructure owner had no control over speech, the telephone network functioned as a neutral conduit for the communication of subscribers. Treating the telephone company as a carrier of other's speech, rather than as a speaker itself, reinforced a regulatory framework that stressed access and nondiscrimination. The FCC required telephone companies to offer transmission facilities for resale to competitive ISPs under reasonable rates and terms, a policy that was grounded in regulatory distinctions originally applied to basic telecommunications and enhanced computer-processing services (U.S. FCC, "Amendment of Section 64.702" 417–23). These access requirements led to a flourishing of ISPs and a diversity of uses and applications. As many note, an underlying infrastructure mandated by law early on to be open and nondiscriminatory became a key feature of the Internet (Feld 39; Hart, Reed, and Bar 667; Lessig, *Future of Ideas* 44–45; Werbach 7).

The chief difference between the broadband and narrowband Internet is one of degree (the speed at which information travels), rather than kind. Nevertheless, the desire to speed the development of broadband services was the impetus for a reconsideration of the regulatory framework that applied to the Internet. The 1996 Telecommunications Act helped to destabilize existing regulatory regimes. The act sought to give major infrastructure providers, particularly cable and telephone companies, incentives to invest in competitive broadband systems, but was largely silent about how to regulate these systems. By liberalizing market entry, reducing cross-market entry barriers, and relaxing concentration and merger rules, the 1996 act encouraged different infrastructure providers to invade each other's markets in order to provide competing packages of information and telecommunication services. The act gambled that by inviting formerly separate industries into one another's markets a new landscape would emerge in which numerous facilities-based competitors offered a range of overlapping services. Intermedia competition would lead to lower overall prices, increased innovation, and investment in a broadband infrastructure. While the act liberalized communications markets, it did not specify a regulatory regime for the broadband networks it hoped to create. At the same time, the government's vision of the Internet was taking shape as one of a fully private network to which it would contribute a stable legal framework and some consumer safeguards (Aufderheide, *Communications Policy* 43, 61).

This policy vacuum has left the speech rights pertaining to the broadband Internet, including those of owners, ISPs, and end users, to evolve along with the networks themselves. Yet, the rights of those who own broadband networks, the terms and conditions under which they operate, and their degree of openness are critical policy questions for the twenty-first century. The Internet may well be the central communication infrastructure of the twenty-first century, and whether people have access to broadband services will most likely determine their ability to participate in the network. Common-carriage regulation, nondiscriminatory access principles, and the presence of multiple ISPs created a relatively affordable and open environment on the narrowband Internet and engendered numerous speaking opportunities. Whether these conditions prevail on the broadband Internet depends in large measure on how these networks take shape, how they are regulated, and whether speech rights are operative there.

The question of infrastructure owner speech rights arose when cable companies began providing Internet services in the late 1990s. Cable Internet service, in which the local cable-television network serves as a community-wide broadband network that connects subscribers to the Internet, has a clear lead in the market for broadband subscribers. The twenty largest cable and telephone firms provide 98 percent of the lines carrying broadband services into the home, more than three-fourths of which are cable lines (U.S. FCC, "Availability of Advanced Telecommunications" 20568). However, unlike the open networks that had long characterized the telephone companies, cable companies pursue a more controlled model of Internet service, in part due to the limited capacity of cable lines to carry bandwidth-intensive communication upstream from end users. Consumer advocates, ISPs, some high-tech businesses, a few local governments, and others have criticized the business plans and practices of major cable Internet providers. Critics charge that cable's preferred approach to the Internet is that of a "walled garden," in which the cable Internet service keeps users within the confines of approved content and applications, restricts content diversity, forecloses opportunities to speak on the network, and stifles competition, innovation, and consumer choice. In response, many communities mandated that cable operators provide third-party access to their broadband infrastructure, sparking law and policy debates over how to regulate broadband Internet services and whether infrastructure owners have speech rights over these systems.[12]

Critics argue that the inclinations of some cable operators to set limits on the ability of end users to send video, to steer customers toward affiliated sites and away from competing sites, to prohibit end users from operating their own web sites and servers, to provide speedier access to affiliated and favored sites, to allocate more bandwidth to content and applications coming from preferred sources, to filter data and communication used for file sharing and other disapproved purposes, and to select one or two affiliated or favored ISPs to provide access to the system harm the values of openness and access online.[13] Others note that, in addition to designing their systems to enable such controls and discrimination, some cable companies implement restrictive subscriber agreements specifying acceptable and unacceptable network usage. Some agreements prohibit the use of corporate networks that enable people to telecommute; bar end users from adding servers, game boxes, or other hardware to the networks; or ban customer access to sites requiring a high level of bandwidth (Krim). Motivated in part by technical limitations, such policies also represent rational business decisions on the part of cable operators. Yet, the walled-garden approach limits the ability of end users to act as information providers and to receive the diversity of information available on the Internet. It also contributes to an unequal topography of information flows. A superhighway comes into the home, but only a narrow pathway leads out. Irrespective of whether these practices are technologically or economically motivated, the cable example shows that such controls are possible. Cities believed that municipal access requirements, forcing cable operators to open their networks, were necessary to address these problems.

Cable Internet-access requirements raised the question of what speech-rights regime should apply to cable Internet services. Cable operators claimed that municipal access requirements violated their speech rights and impinged on their ability to control communication over their systems. They argued that access requirements constituted "forced access" to networks over which they have legitimate speech rights, provided disincentives for investing in broadband, and exceeded the regulatory powers of municipal cable-franchising authorities. Cities saw these requirements as necessary to protect access to an essential communication facility, competition among ISPs, and the nondiscriminatory character of the Internet (*AT&T v. City of Portland* [1999] 1150).

District courts analyzing the First Amendment dimensions of cable Internet access came to contradictory conclusions. Although subsequently overturned for reasons unrelated to speech rights, the 1999 district court case *AT&T v. City of Portland* endorsed access requirements for cable Internet operators. The court viewed the access rules as content-neutral regulations that did not infringe on cable-operator speech rights (1154). The rules did not discriminate against speech or require cable Internet operators to carry particular messages. Instead, the rules furthered a substantial government interest in encouraging competition on the Internet over cable and narrowly regulated speech to achieve that interest. For the court, the creation of access rights was a legitimate government undertaking that did not contravene the First Amendment. In contrast to the empowering approach of *AT&T v. City of Portland,* the district court in *Comcast Cablevision of Broward v. Broward County* employed a defensive speech-rights framework to argue that the First Amendment prevented the government from mandating access to the Internet over cable. Although Broward County had sought to level the playing field among competitors and to give citizens access to diverse ISPs, the access rules violated Comcast's First Amendment right to determine programming on their system (*Comcast Cablevision* 686). Invoking *Miami Herald,* the Supreme Court case that struck down a right of access to newspapers, the court argued that access rights necessarily inhibit free speech by interfering with the editorial discretion of cable Internet operators (*Comcast Cablevision* 694). The *Comcast Cablevision* court invoked First Amendment absolutism and a literal reading of the phrase "Congress shall make no law" to support exclusive speech rights for cable Internet operators (695).

Although these district court cases explicitly addressed the question of infrastructure-owner speech rights, later cases and policy discussions recast the debate in terms of categorizing the type of technological services involved. Two federal appeals court cases, *AT&T v. City of Portland* (2000) and *MediaOne Group v. County of Henrico* (2001), struck down the access rules, but declined to consider the speech-rights implications of their decisions. These courts found that cable Internet service involves a telecommunication component, which cities do not have jurisdiction to regulate. Although telecommunication services normally operate under common-carriage principles that assign speech rights and speaker status to system users, rather than to system owners, the courts reserved judgment on how lawmakers should regulate these services, essentially deferring to the FCC, who had so far followed a de facto policy of inaction.

Shortly after these cases, the FCC stated its approach to broadband services. The agency argued that regulatory forbearance was necessary to spur investment in broadband networks and speed their diffusion. In a declaratory ruling, the FCC asserted that under the 1996 Telecommunications Act cable Internet service was an information service that the FCC could choose to regulate, rather than a telecommunications service that required common-carriage regulation (U.S. FCC, "High-Speed Access to the Internet" 4802).[14] However, the 9th Circuit Court of Appeals disagreed. In 2003 the appeals court reaffirmed the *AT&T v. City of Portland* decision in *Brand X Internet Services v. FCC,* saying that cable Internet services are both information and telecommunication services. Although the debate had become one of classifications, it implicitly raised the question of whether speech rights apply to the network infrastructure, since information service owners presumably have speech rights while telecommunication service owners do not.

The question of how to treat broadband Internet service came before the Supreme Court in 2005 in *National Cable and Telecommunications Association v. Brand X Internet Services.* Rather than consider the ramifications of different models of broadband regulation for free speech on the Internet, the Court focused on whether the earlier *Brand X Internet Services v. FCC* ruling improperly rejected the FCC's categorization of cable Internet service as an information, rather than a telecommunication, service. Instead of accepting the FCC's categorization, the appeals court had privileged its own earlier ruling in *AT&T v. City of Portland,* which had determined that cable Internet service was both an information and telecommunication service. The Supreme Court reversed this opinion, holding that courts could reject only agency constructions of statutes that were so clear that they foreclosed all other interpretations (*Brand X Internet Services v. FCC* 2700). The 1996 Telecommunications Act defined information services as those "offering . . . a capability for [processing] information via telecommunications" and telecommunications service as those "offering . . . telecommunications for a fee directly to the public" (47 US Code sec. 153(20)(46), cited in *Brand X Internet Services v. FCC* 2698). The Court accepted the FCC's argument that these definitions were ambiguous, as well as its interpretation of their meaning. According to the FCC, although cable Internet service actually provides both information and telecommunication services, it cannot be said to "offer" both services from the perspective of the consumer. For the consumer, the telecommunication component merely aids in the provision of the primary service "offered," which is an information service (2703–4). The Court also noted that the FCC had rightly concluded that a minimal regulatory environment would better promote investment in the broadband marketplace (2711).

In effect, the Court sanctioned a neoliberal policy approach to broadband services that privileged facilitating marketplace competition and regulatory restraint over free-speech concerns. Although the dissent accused the FCC of using an implausible reading of the statute in order to achieve broadband deregulation, it also failed to raise any of the free-speech issues implicated by the case (2713).

The FCC's position is problematic in several respects. Its interpretation turned on what it presumed the consumer thought was offered, rather than the actual components of the product. The FCC refused to acknowledge that the primary difference between broadband and narrowband Internet service from the user's point of view is probably the speed at which information travels, which is a function of the underlying technology. The FCC's position was also inconsistent. According to the commission, Internet access through narrowband services, like dial-up, is both a telecommunication and an information service—and therefore subject to some common-carriage regulation. Yet, the same Internet access through broadband services is an information service only—and therefore exempt from common-carriage regulation. In reality, the only difference between the two is the speed at which a user may receive or send information. Finally, the FCC's actions are unlikely to further their own goal of promoting competition in the marketplace. By successfully petitioning to overturn municipal requirements that cable operators provide competing ISPs access to their networks, the FCC has dramatically reduced the number of broadband providers available to consumers and thereby vitiated the cornerstone of the marketplace approach to regulation—open competition.

Shortly after the *Brand X* decision, the FCC announced that telephone-based broadband Internet services would receive the same regulatory treatment as cable (U.S. FCC, "Appropriate Framework for Broadband Access over Wireline Facilities"). The FCC's intent was to spur investment in the broadband infrastructure by providing a level playing field for these two dominant infrastructure providers (Hearn; Schatz). Although the Court did not consider the speech-rights implications of the *Brand X* decision, the consequences of classifying infrastructure owners as information services are clear. Unlike common carriers, the courts consider ISPs to be proprietary owners of the systems they control and the primary speakers over these systems. Although the FCC has suggested that it can still apply principles of nondiscrimination and neutrality to these information services, if it so chooses (U.S. FCC, "Inquiry concerning High-Speed Access"; U.S. FCC, "Appropriate Framework for Broadband Access over Wireline Facilities"), such regulations are unlikely to withstand First Amendment challenges if infrastructure owners are not classified as common carriers. If Congress allows the FCC's approach to prevail, the future of free speech online will depend on whether other technologies can gain enough momentum to proffer significant competition to the cable and telephone providers who currently dominate the market.

A better approach would be for government to ensure free speech online by mandating neutrality principles and common-carrier requirements, to the extent that they are technically feasible, on the underlying network infrastructure. Applying principles of nondiscrimination, neutrality, and access and treating the broadband infrastructure as a common carrier for speech-rights purposes prevents infrastructure owners from leveraging their control over vital communication pipelines into control over the information and ideas that their lines transmit. It also reduces the likelihood that some communities would have as little as two access providers to choose from—the phone or the cable company—when subscribing to broadband Internet services, or at best three or four providers ("Net Losses?"; "Strike Up the Broadband"). Few choices among Internet-access services run the risk of empowering broadband providers to exercise discriminatory controls over access, to manipulate information flows, and to raise rates. According infrastructure owners speech rights online—and then failing to apply principles of openness and nondiscrimination—may facilitate a transformation of the Internet away from a space for democratic communication toward one in which only owners have the right and can define the opportunities to speak.

The Internet, Public Space, and Private Prerogative

In many ways, the Internet feels and functions like a public space. Large parts of the network operate free from government coercion and commercial pressure. Outside of libraries and schools, the government has been unable to censor speech on the network. Through a combination of regulation, competition, and cooperation, the Internet has thus far kept commercial pressures at bay. Commercial online services with links to the Internet often don the mantle of open and inclusive communities (Mitchell 129). The software that runs the Internet also has a public dimension. In a model of public and private cooperation, the different networks that comprise the Internet voluntarily use TCP/IP protocols to interconnect with one another. An artifact of the public spirit of the early Internet, TCP/IP embodies an open-source model of software programming. The knowledge needed to write programs that run on the network is open and nonproprietary, and people can contribute new applications, services, and components without the permission of network owners or gatekeepers (Cooper 1018; Hart, Reed, and Bar 683; Mitchell 169). Open protocols create a commons on top of an otherwise controlled infrastructure (Lessig, *Future of Ideas* 176). Yet, the conditions that create the aura of public space, as well as many of the opportunities for free speech, are changing. While the basic telephone networks that form the core infrastructure of much Internet communication still function as common carriers, the FCC has exempted both cable and telephone companies from common-carriage requirements for their broadband networks. It is unlikely that, as Internet-access providers, these companies will operate with the same degree of openness as the thousands of competitive ISPs that have preceded them. Many predict that in the future a paucity of infrastructure-affiliated ISPs will act as restrictive gatekeepers to the broadband Internet. Unlike the highly competitive ISPs of the past, these ISPs will be less likely to provide Internet access at a low cost or with the same equality of service, including first-come, first-served transaction processing and few deliberate constraints on network bandwidth.

Equally significantly, while the Internet may feel like a public space, legally it is not a public space, nor is it likely to become one under current public-forum law. Public-forum law creates zones for free speech where the public's right to speak is primary. Neither the government nor private actors can censor speech in public forums. As we have seen, the interpretive tradition in public-forum law works against granting public-forum status to new media or to any media that are privately owned or operated. While the status of a traditional public forum accords only to public property that has long been held open to the public, designated public forums are limited to public property dedicated to expression. Some lower courts emphatically deny that the Internet meets the criteria for public-forum status. Both *Cyber v. AOL* and *CompuServe v. Cyber* held that privately owned servers and networks are not public forums over which end users have the right to speak. Citing *Lloyd v. Tanner*, these courts agreed that public-forum law applies only to public property or to property that takes on all the characteristics of a municipality. The *Cyber v. AOL* court ruled that AOL is neither a traditional nor a designated public forum. The court acknowledged that, as a site where millions of people exchange information and ideas, the Internet has some public characteristics. Nevertheless, neither AOL nor the broader Internet is government run, exercises a full range of municipal powers, or provides public services traditionally offered by the state. AOL is a private company that makes its services available to customers for a fee, said the court, not a public system subject to First Amendment prohibitions. In these cases, the courts argued that the many private actors who connect to the Internet retain their right to exclude unwanted speech and speakers from their property. In *US v. ALA,* the Supreme Court held that even Internet access provided through public libraries could not be considered a traditional or designated public forum. The Court reasoned that the Internet is a recent phenomenon, not one that has "immemorially been held in trust for the use of the public" (232). Additionally, libraries offer Internet access not in order to provide a public forum, but simply as another way of making information available, and to treat library Internet access as public forums would conflict with the role of libraries as cultural arbiters (232–33).

As the above cases suggest, the Internet is a site of conflict over public and private rights. This conflict stems from the Internet's uneasy blend of public- and private-network elements and functions. Though it may feel like a public space to many of its users, the Internet is made up of a multitude of interconnected networks. Many of these are private, such as those belonging to commercial ISPs and private company intranets, which serve a closed membership even as they rely on public carrier facilities.[15] Others are public networks, like those run by libraries and schools. There are also the privately owned, but publicly regulated, telephone networks that interconnect with the majority of these subnetworks. In a communication marketplace ruled by neoliberal views of private-property rights, infrastructure owners and gatekeepers possess the right to control how others use their property, regardless of whether it has a public function. They decide who does and does not have access, set the terms of service for network users, and monitor and control information flows. Under this philosophy, network owners have the legal right to construct closed and proprietary systems. Whether these owners design their networks to serve democratic values like free speech is their prerogative, and the public has no right to speak over these systems. In a highly competitive marketplace where interconnection, interoperability, equality of service, and reasonable and affordable terms of service are the norm, democratic communication on the Internet can thrive. Many argue, however, that these conditions will vanish in a market where increasingly concentrated private companies have absolute control over their networks (Benkler, "Property" 22; Colby 136; Lessig, *Code* 221). To the extent that competitive conditions have been met in the past, much of the credit goes to government regulations that have kept the core infrastructure open and accessible. In the future, unchecked private-market actors may choose not to support the conditions that have been so conducive to democratic communication. While market regulation may encourage the private sector to develop the network, the costs of this in terms of free speech and public space is too high.

The Internet today constitutes a potential forum for democratic communication. It serves a number of public functions, including carrying e-mail, hosting bulletin boards and list services, and publishing news and information. Whether it will support democratic communication in the future will depend in part on what model of regulation applies, the extent to which the government permits network owners and gatekeepers to control access and content, and the level of competition remaining in the system. The FCC and other proponents of market regulation anticipate that unmitigated property rights for telecommunications providers will foster open, competitive, and decentralized media systems (U.S. FCC, "Inquiry Concerning High-Speed Access"; Pool, *Technologies of Freedom* 236; U.S. FCC, "Notice of Proposed Rulemaking"). Short of monopoly or duopoly conditions in which one or two players dominate the market, the Internet does not require regulation to encourage competition or interconnection. Critics of this neoliberal approach counter that absolute property rights are more likely to do harm than good. If given the opportunity, dominant infrastructure owners, including cable and telephone companies, will exert control over the network (Benkler, "Net Regulation" 1237; Geller 36). Furthermore, the critics see oligopoly conditions where a handful of dominant players control the market, much less one or two, as equally damaging to the public interest and necessitating government intervention (Feld 40). Government action, in their view, should instill free-speech values and genuine public spaces into the overall structure of the Internet.

Achieving a Democratic Internet

Democratic communication on the Internet requires a network structure that allows end users to produce, exchange, and obtain information. In other words, users must have the capability to act as both information senders and receivers. Democratic communication also calls for universally available public spaces that privilege social and political discourse free from pressures of both the government and private enterprise. There are several ways that the government could protect democratic communication on the Internet. Finding the best way will be a matter of experimentation and careful monitoring. However, the foremost policy concern should be to maintain and maximize principles of openness and nondiscrimination to basic network resources, including infrastructure and bandwidth. These principles are fundamental to democratic communication on the Internet and need to be privileged regardless of whether the network is publicly or privately owned and operated.

National policy historically facilitated democratic conditions on the Internet, founded as it was on a ubiquitous telephone network governed by principles of common carriage and nondiscriminatory access. These principles can be carried over to broadband networks. Accessible, equitable, and open networks are achievable with content-neutral government regulations that prevent network owners from exerting complete control over core elements of the network infrastructure. Regulation can extend the values of interconnection, nondiscriminatory access, interoperability, and reasonable terms of service to any telecommunications or wireless infrastructure provider. At a minimum, such regulations can apply to a portion of the provider's carrying capacity, ensuring some spaces for free speech. Although the FCC has chosen not to impose common-carriage regulation on the broadband Internet infrastructure, Congress can and should do so in its next set of revisions to communications policy. Hearings on revisions to the 1996 Telecommunications Act have already begun, and the future regulatory framework of broadband services was one of the first items on the agenda.

Many policy analysts have argued that strong common-carriage rules, or at least associated principles such as neutral interconnection and interoperability, offer the only means of discouraging network owners from exerting control over access and content (Colby 169; Cooper 1068; Geller; Noam 451). Broadly applied, common-carriage principles could reinforce neutral interconnection and interoperability throughout the network, prevent infrastructure owners from acting as network gatekeepers, and ensure that the network as a whole functions as an open space. Multiple advantages adhere to this approach. Uniform and consistent regulations would maintain network openness across all infrastructure providers, including cable, DSL, wireless, and any other platform that emerges. Although a blanket marketplace approach would also have consistency, market regulation encourages closed systems with financial incentives for network providers to favor their own content over the content of others. Open systems, on the other hand, cannot leverage their control over conduit into control over potential speakers or speech. Ownership rights, in this case, would not include the right to censor content or to limit access to one or two affiliated ISPs. While infrastructure owners like local telephone or cable companies could provide access through their own ISP, they would also have to allow others onto their systems. Common-carriage regulation would apply to the system infrastructure, but not to individual ISPs. Common-carriage rules are neutral structural regulations that decentralize the production and distribution of information while precluding the possibility of both government and market control. In an environment with only a handful of competitive platforms, common-carriage rules, along with neutrality, access, and interconnection provisions, preserve the maximum amount of competition among ISPs.

The above options require public regulation of privately owned property. There are ample precedents for such regulation in communication history. Yet, as we have seen, they are sites of perpetual conflict over speech rights. A third alternative for a democratic Internet tries to overcome these conflicts by creating public spaces on public property, or sites that unambiguously qualify as legal public forums. One option is for government policy to guarantee network openness by creating a public infrastructure dedicated to free expression. For instance, publicly owned ISPs that build broadband connections to the home could operate as public forums. These government-sponsored networks would privilege the speech rights of end users, operate according to public values and principles, and prohibit government and commercial censorship. However, the public funding of such networks would require significant capital outlays, which is why many in government prefer to encourage the private sector to finance the development of broadband networks. In addition, the telephone industry has successfully lobbied numerous states to pass bills that prevent local governments from offering telecommunications services, and in 2004 the U.S. Supreme Court upheld the right of states to pass this legislation (*Nixon v. Missouri Municipal League*). Congress should protect municipal broadband by prohibiting legislation that preempts the rights of local governments to decide for themselves whether to develop their own broadband networks.

Conclusion

In the United States and elsewhere, the law, policy, economics, and design of computer networks are evolving. Changes along one or more of these axes could precipitate a transformation in the conditions surrounding communication on the Internet. Speech-rights law will play an important role in how the Internet evolves. Laws that threaten to censor speech or place substantial burdens on network participants are likely to face First Amendment scrutiny. The regulatory framework chosen by the government for the broadband Internet infrastructure will help determine who has a right to speak in these spaces. Private-sector actors that alter the nondiscriminatory, open, and equitable character of the network can do so only if granted absolute speech rights over these systems. Those harmed by these changes, including independent ISPs, end users, and others who are denied interconnection, refused access, or otherwise limited in what and how they can communicate, may fight for their speech rights over these forums. To date, the claims of users have held little force against the private-property rights of commercial online services, ISPs, and infrastructure owners and managers to control speech on their networks and services, and even ISPs may have no rights against owners of the underlying network.

The defensive approach to speech rights is a fierce guard against government intrusion on Internet speech in private spaces. In this approach, freedom of speech exists as long as the government refrains from acting in the private sphere, and the primary justification for government action is a narrow definition of market failure. This approach ties speech rights to private-property ownership. Speech rights belong to those who control the means to speak, not to the broader public. While the public has a right to speak on public property that constitutes a public forum, this right does not extend to media that involve a mix of public and private infrastructures, protocols, and functions. The Internet is made up of both public and private networks, and most people access the system through private ISPs. Consequently, the defensive approach permits infrastructure owners and ISPs to control speech, should they choose, at the expense of network end users.

Policies that promote access, interconnection, and the speech rights of end users cannot survive a purely defensive speech regime. If the Internet is to remain receptive to democratic communication, First Amendment law must permit government to preserve the conditions necessary to the exercise of speech rights. Empowering speech rights recognize that democratic communication depends on more than government inaction. It requires affordable and accessible media that allow everyone to send and receive communication at least some of the time. Achieving democratic communication on the Internet also necessitates the existence of network space insulated from commercial pressures and government coercion. This space can exist on both public and private networks, as long as these maintain the conditions necessary to democratic communication. In an empowering regime, the government must not harm or abridge speech, but it can implement neutral laws and policies that protect the speech rights of the broader citizenry. This approach focuses on the public functions and responsibilities of the media in democratic societies and does not equate speech rights solely with property ownership or management. From this perspective, ownership rights do not necessarily include absolute control over network access and content. The government can subject owners to structural regulations aimed at cultivating an environment that supports democratic communication.

Law and policy set the parameters for democratic communication on the Internet by establishing a basic regulatory framework that governs the network. This framework involves social choices about the values shaping the space, the terms and conditions of network access, and the availability and allocation of network resources. Lawmakers considering speech rights on the Internet should not reify the network or forget the government's role in creating this sphere for democratic communication. The Internet is an amalgamation of public and private network elements layered on top of existing network infrastructures, including telephone, wireless, and cable technology. Its foundation has been publicly regulated telephone networks that provide nondiscriminatory interconnection on reasonable terms and conditions and that have no prerogative to control speech on their systems. Future regulatory frameworks can enhance the democratic potential of the Internet or decimate it. Speech-rights law should help sustain democratic communication networks by supporting policy initiatives designed to foster free speech and to prevent the delimitation of speech by a paucity of network owners and ISPs and by the government.

6   The Future of Democratic Communication

HOW OUR LEGAL SYSTEM INTERPRETS speech rights in the media has profound consequences for democratic communication. Simply having the First
Amendment in the U.S. Constitution does not guarantee the protection of
citizens' speech rights. Rather, it is how the courts understand and apply the
First Amendment that shapes the actual rights and realities of the majority
of people wishing to communicate. Every interpretation of speech rights is
based on a theory of democracy. In the United States, different First Amendment interpretations draw on a range of interconnected ideas that stem from
divergent traditions within democratic liberalism. These include ideas about
the nature of rights, the definition of freedom, the realm in which freedom is
operative, sources of coercion, the role of the state in protecting rights, and
conditions under which citizens can exercise freedom. How courts interpret
the First Amendment has real effects on democratic life, either resulting in
actual opportunities to communicate or stripping the public of these opportunities. Moreover, courts can alter and transform legal understandings
of speech rights by adopting different views of liberal-democratic theory.
Speech-rights interpretations often turn on whether the courts follow the
tenets of neoliberal or participatory-democratic theory.

Achieving democratic speech rights, and ultimately a more democratic
society, is a multipronged task. At a fundamental level, it demands the adoption of a theory of democracy that offers the majority of people adequate
opportunities to engage in discourse and deliberation with one another. The
defensive theory of democratic speech rights that presently dominates U.S.
policy and politics cannot do the job. Participatory-democratic theory points

out serious flaws in this quintessentially neoliberal approach. Insensitive to the real-world conditions that affect speech opportunities, concerned almost exclusively with protecting private rather than public spheres, hemmed in by a negative definition of freedom, and immobilized by an overly restrictive view of state action, the defensive approach provides an unsatisfactory interpretation of the First Amendment. As I have argued throughout this book, participatory-democratic theory offers not only the best account of the role of communication in democratic societies, but also a more satisfactory reading of the terms and tenets of democratic liberalism. An empowering approach is what's needed to secure the conditions necessary to democratic communication on both old and new media.

A more democratic understanding of speech rights requires not only a frank assessment of the shortcomings of current First Amendment law, but also the acceptance and application of policy principles rooted in participatory-democratic thought. In this final chapter, I review the meaning and status of free speech today and offer an alternative set of policy principles for guiding future interpretations of speech rights. These principles offer baseline protections for democratic speech rights and, taken together, support a favorable legal foundation upon which myriad experiments in democratic communication can flourish.

The Meaning of Free Speech in the United States

As the *Red Lion, CBS v. DNC, Miami Herald, Denver Area,* and *US v. ALA* cases show, the Court has given far less protection to democratic communication in today's popular media than in the unmediated forums of communication granted broad speech-rights protections in the 1930s. Consequently, while ordinary citizens have exercisable speech rights in public places, such as streets and parks, they have virtually no right to speak in the dominant communications forums of contemporary society. As Kairys points out, modern definitions of speech rights are more appropriate to an antiquated period in which assembling, speaking, and disseminating literature in public places were major modes of communication (261). These definitions are poorly suited to a time when democratic communication effectively takes place through mediated channels.

Democratic communication demands that the public have real opportunities to articulate and exchange insights about its experience of the social world. This process, known as social mediation, requires at a minimum the right to send and receive communication in spaces that are free from market and government coercion alike. Yet, the legal cases examined here reveal that the Supreme Court has failed by and large to support these conditions in privately owned and managed media. In the cases of the 1960s and 1970s, the Court refused to grant the public full speech rights in the single-channel media of print and broadcast, secured the public only a very limited right to receive information in broadcast, and effectively rejected its right to send and receive information in print. The Court objected to narrowly drawn right-of-reply and access rules contained in such policies as a right of reply for political candidates in print and a proposed right of access to broadcast advertising space. Arguing that such policies were content based or interfered with the absolute editorial discretion of media owners, the Court found them to be unlawful infringements on the First Amendment rights of the media. Thus, the Court upheld speech rights against what it saw as incursions by the state, but not against the potential restrictions on the public by media owners or market forces.

These cases left open the possibility that less intrusive access policies might withstand legal scrutiny. However, the Court's failure to extend First Amendment protection to democratic communication forums on multichannel media, represented by public-access cable television, reveal an animosity toward access rights that extend beyond their particular structure. Congress designed public-access channels specifically to overcome the Court's previous objections toward access policies. These channels do not require the government to evaluate the performance of the cable operator. Moreover, they are content neutral in that cable-operator speech does not trigger their existence. As one House Report noted, public-access channels were "narrowly drawn structural regulations" designed to "ensure a diversity of information sources without government intrusion into the content of programming carried on the system" (U.S. Congress: House, *Cable Franchise Policy* 35). Although the Court has allowed access channels to carry on through local franchise agreements, it has yet to grant these channels and their users substantive First Amendment protections. Its failure to do so is the result of a largely defensive approach to speech rights.

Although the Supreme Court has yet to formulate a comprehensive speech regime for computer networks, it has prevented the government from censoring producers of Internet content in what it saw as an ideal speech environment online and has allowed censorship of end users who access the Internet through the public library. In addition, numerous lower court decisions imply that private-sector actors, unlike the government, will have wide latitude in controlling information and content that flow over computer networks. If these cases are indicative of future legal reasoning, system owners and operators who own or run proprietary equipment and services will possess speech rights on these systems, while network end users will not. Clients, customers, and employees who use these facilities and services must abide by the terms and conditions set by these system gatekeepers, which the courts view as the real speakers online. If a defensive approach to online communication prevails, the ability of end users to find adequate opportunities for democratic communication will depend on the extent to which services and technology remain competitive and network owners and gatekeepers choose to control content, access, and services; government will have little leeway to structure these conditions.

Rooted in neoliberal-democratic theory, the defensive approach entrains several assumptions that are hostile to a public right of media access. First, under this approach, any government regulation of speech in private spheres and spaces abridges the First Amendment rights of media owners. This approach understands public and private property as distinct and fixed categories. It does not recognize that private property may have public functions or that spaces may be quasipublic. The defensive approach views all government policies, even those that are content neutral and nondiscriminatory or that work to expand speech opportunities, as unlawful intrusions on the proprietary rights of private-property owners. Thus, the *Miami Herald* Court struck down a right-of-reply statute for newspapers in part because it saw no difference between regulations that censored the media and those that created additional speaking opportunities for the public. Similarly, Justice Thomas argued in *Denver Area* that public-access channels constituted the forced speech of the cable operator, rather than the free speech of the public. Since all government regulation of the private realm is censorship in this view, the government can never have a compelling reason to implement policies that promote the democratic communications interests of the public over private media or that serve as an antidote to marketplace conditions that constrain speech. When applied to computer networks, this approach suggests that the First Amendment would also prohibit the government from regulating access to the Internet (*Comcast Cablevision*). Moreover, as *US v. ALA* shows, its exclusive focus on private spaces as the realm of freedom leaves neoliberalism ill equipped to recognize public spaces in which speech rights should be operative.

Second, conditions that constrain speech outside of government censorship of speech in private spaces are irrelevant to considerations of speech rights. Since the state is the only serious threat to democratic communication, the law need only defend speech rights against state actors and not against other coercive agents, such as marketplace actors. Hence, while the *Miami Herald* Court acknowledges that the newspaper industry may be highly concentrated, monopolistic, and anticompetitive and that most citizens have no voice in the press, it regards these facts as irrelevant for determining free-speech rights in print. In deliberating over the fate of public-access cable channels, the *Denver Area* Court upholds current arrangements for reasons of custom and tradition. It does not invoke the obvious economic and structural factors that might also justify cable-access policies, such as the monopoly status of most local cable systems or the cable operator's control of numerous channels into the home. Finally, while the *CBS v. DNC* Court, following *Red Lion,* agrees that market failure based on broadcast spectrum scarcity justifies some speech-rights protections for the public in broadcasting, it bases its reasoning not on the economic conditions of the broadcast market but on the notion that the government cannot unduly favor some speakers over others when licensing broadcast spectrum. In other words, these cases protect the public's right to receive information not simply because the market fails to provide ample opportunities to broadcast, but because law and policy must reconcile the government's role in licensing broadcasters with prohibitions against government censorship.

A third assumption of the defensive approach is that the absolute editorial control of media owners serves the interests of the public at large. In this view, the media owner possesses the only legitimate speaking interest over media, and speech rights are safe only so long as the law protects the media owner's ability to speak. Thus, the *Miami Herald* Court assumes that as long as it can shield newspapers from government access policies, free speech is secure in print. While the more empowering *Red Lion* Court acknowledges that the public has it own speech interest in broadcasting, the Court understands this interest as a right to receive information only. Building on this line of reasoning, the *CBS v. DNC* Court holds that the broadcaster's absolute control over content and exclusive representation of the public interest best serves the public's speech rights. In all of these cases, the Court presumes that the protection of media-owner speech provides adequate protection for speech rights generally. In *US v. ALA,* the Court gives the government sponsors of library Internet access the same power to speak as print and broadcast media owners. According to the Court, the government's role as a cultural arbiter effaces the speech rights of Internet users in public libraries.

Finally, this approach not only leads the Court to identify the speech rights of media owners with the broader public interest, but also to equate the speech rights of citizens with narrow special interests. From this perspective, public access to the media harms the public interest and results in public control and manipulation of media content. In *Miami Herald,* the Court argues that a public right of access would result in less, rather than more, speech because it would chill the newspaper's incentive to speak. The *CBS v. DNC* Court carried this assumption to its logical extreme, arguing that even a limited public right to speak during commercial airtime would strip broadcasters of their editorial control, prevent them from acting as public trustees, and enable wealthy members of the public to dominate political agendas. The Court identifies a right of access to the media, no matter how circumscribed, with the unbridled control of media content by special interests.

Policies that seek to create or expand public speech opportunities in the media cannot survive under a purely defensive regime. According to this approach, democratic societies should leave speech-rights determinations to competitive markets, which it sees as neutral and noncoercive distributors of communication resources. Over the past few decades, U.S. communication policy has undergone a transition from a public-trustee approach to a marketplace approach for achieving social goals. Relying on new technologies and market competition, proponents of deregulation assume that democratic communication will thrive in private spaces absent government intervention. Yet, if speech rights on computer networks or other new technologies are interpreted defensively, media owners and managers could circumscribe and control speaking opportunities on new media. Coupled with the Supreme Court's generally defensive approach to speech rights, deregulatory policy has left citizens with few guaranteed outlets for democratic communication in contemporary media.

Alternative Policy Principles for Democratic Speech Rights

Participatory-democratic theory, with its empowering view of speech rights, offers a viable alternative to the defensive approach. From this perspective, market conditions that inhibit widespread speaking opportunities justify government regulations that promote speech rights. Although the law should not permit the government to censor speech, it can allow government to implement content-neutral policies that protect the conditions necessary for democratic communication. First Amendment law has been largely, though not entirely, successful at protecting people from government coercion, but the communication needs of democratic societies require that the law expand to provide similar protections from equally coercive market mechanisms. Under an empowering regime, the public's speech rights include the right to both send and receive communication. In addition, people must find opportunities to communicate in the real socioeconomic context of modern media. In this regime, public access to the media serves the public interest because it enables people to exercise their speech rights, while absolute control over content by a limited number of media owners is contrary to the public interest.

The future of democratic communication depends on the adoption of an alternative set of policy principles to guide decisions about speech rights. These principles, drawn from the central tenets of participatory-democratic theory, are necessary to safeguard and support an empowering view of speech rights and a more democratic communication environment. These principles are that the government has a compelling interest in promoting democratic communication, the courts must interpret the First Amendment in light of real social conditions, the media have a public function in democratic societies, and hybrid regulatory models are an acceptable means of protecting democratic communication in contemporary media. An elaboration of these points will demonstrate that they are well within the purview of liberal-democratic theory and have ample legal precedent to support them.

The Government Has a Compelling Interest in Promoting Democratic Communication

Participatory-democratic theory asserts that the state has a duty to protect and promote democratic communication. Although it recognizes that the law must prevent the state from censoring speech, participatory theory also acknowledges the state's role as an agent of the public. As such, the public may call upon the state to protect its rights from other coercive forces. In this view, the state has both a positive obligation and a compelling interest to ensure that opportunities and forums for democratic communication are available. While the government must refrain from stifling free speech, it must also be able to intervene to eliminate other nongovernmental threats to free speech and to affirmatively support openings and occasions for expression. From this vantage point, government regulations that expand speech opportunities within media comport, rather than conflict, with the First Amendment.

The notion that the government has a compelling interest in maintaining resources and institutions for democratic communication is a critical starting point for reforming First Amendment law. Indeed, the courts routinely test the constitutionality of media regulation by making reference to legal standards that contain a government-interest clause. The two most commonly invoked standards are known as the "intermediate scrutiny" and "strict scrutiny" tests. The strict-scrutiny test states that for a content-based regulation to survive, the government must have designed it as narrowly as possible to serve a compelling government interest. While the courts apply the strict-scrutiny test to content-based regulations of speech in public forums, they use the intermediate-scrutiny test to evaluate regulations thought to be content neutral. The intermediate-scrutiny test states that content-neutral regulations are constitutional if they are narrowly tailored to serve an important or substantial, rather than a compelling, government interest.

Several cases make clear that the government has a vital interest in protecting democratic communication. Though the concept of a compelling or substantial interest did not exist at the time of *Red Lion*, in its decision to uphold the Fairness Doctrine the Court indicated that the government has a significant interest in supporting policies that protect the public's speech rights from private censorship. The Supreme Court expresses this sentiment in several other decisions, including *Associated Press v. US, Turner Broadcasting System v. FCC* (*Turner I*), and *Turner Broadcasting System v. FCC* (*Turner II*). In *Turner II,* the Court upheld "must carry" rules that required cable television systems to carry local broadcast stations on some of their channels. The *Turner II* Court said that the government has a legitimate interest in maintaining competitive and diverse information sources for the public and in preserving a strong system of free and local broadcast television, particularly for the 40 percent of U.S. households without cable services. In addition, Brennan's dissent in *CBS v. DNC* asserts that the government has a compelling interest in fostering democratic debate and discussion, promoting the dissemination of diverse viewpoints, and creating a public right of access to the media. While *Denver Area* recognizes that the government can create a right of access to cable systems, it neglects to discuss the particular interests that such policies serve. Lower court cases also recognize that the government has a compelling interest in protecting the public's right to send and receive communication. In *Erie Telecommunications v. City of Erie* and

Berkshire Cablevision of Rhode Island v. Burke, the lower courts upheld PEG-access requirements as content-neutral rules that furthered a compelling government interest in the First Amendment rights of viewers and the free flow of information. At least one district court case dealing with computer networks, *AT&T v. City of Portland* (1999), determined that regulations mandating open access on the cable Internet furthered a legitimate government interest in encouraging competition among Internet providers.

The state will not have authority to fully protect speech rights, however, unless lawmakers and policy-makers recognize that state action can promote, as well as proscribe, democratic communication. Lawmakers must recognize that the First Amendment enjoins against laws that "abridge" speech, not all laws having to do with speech. The word "abridge" denotes not any type of action, but only those that diminish or lessen free speech. As I have shown throughout this book, distinguishing between policies and laws that advance or abridge speech is anathema to the defensive approach. Time and again, this approach fails to differentiate between policies that create opportunities for speech and those that censor speech. When they adopt an empowering approach, however, the courts can discern this difference. In *Red Lion,* for example, the Supreme Court determined that some FCC rules enhanced rather than abridged the First Amendment rights of public and press. *Red Lion* held that government policies that do not censor specific programs, prevent broadcasters from expressing themselves, or require them to convey government viewpoints do not abridge broadcasters' freedom of speech. The dissent in *US v. ALA* also uses an empowering approach to distinguish between necessary regulations that raise no free-speech concerns and unnecessary regulations that abridge speech. According to the dissent, regulations that aim to censor materials already in the libraries' possession are unnecessary and illegitimate infringements on the speech rights of library patrons.

To fulfill its mandate under participatory-democratic theory, the state must find ways to regulate without abridging speech whenever extant conditions fail to provide for the exercise of free speech. All media regulation will in some sense influence content. Indeed, the aim of media regulation is often to increase the number of message sources, the diversity of content, or even the quality of content. This influence can, however, operate in ways that are essentially content neutral. Emerson has suggested that the state can regulate speech in constitutionally acceptable ways as long as it enacts laws and policies that are narrowly framed, equitably applied, and objective (*System of Freedom* 634). Another way to navigate the problem is for lawmakers to distinguish between media regulations that apply directly to content and structural regulations that are essentially content neutral. Turow makes the useful distinction between regulations that operate on a content level and those that operate on a structural level (*Media Industries* 17–20). While the content level involves the regulation of specific messages or message policies, the structural level includes regulations that shape organizational processes and relationships within communication industries. Policies that media trigger with the content of their speech or that call on the FCC and the courts to evaluate media content are content level regulations. These policies, however carefully applied, run the risk of inhibiting or chilling freedom of speech and press. Structural regulations incur no such risk. Operating in a content-neutral fashion, structural regulations can protect the speech rights of the public without restricting those of media owners.

The Courts Must Interpret the First Amendment in Light of Real Conditions

The empowering approach to speech rights demands that lawmakers take real conditions into account when deciding conflicts over First Amendment rights. Democratic communication requires that citizens possess the resources and means to exercise their speech rights in the actual media. If they are to support democratic processes, media must act as a mode of expression for the broader citizenry at least some of the time. Justice Brennan underscores this point in his dissent to *CBS v. DNC*. He argues that allowing broadcasters to bar citizen access to the airwaves is unconstitutional because it effectively prevents them from participating in a dominant medium for democratic discussion and debate.

If free speech is to be the right of many, and not just the privilege of a modicum of media owners, governments must be cognizant of all factors that inhibit democratic communication in modern media. As Emerson has suggested, the courts need to interpret the First Amendment in such a way that it creates an effective system of freedom of expression in a given social context (*System of Freedom* 15). In order to maintain a system of free speech, governments must devise a workable structure of principles, practices, institutions, and rights capable of responding to real conditions and achieving predefined goals. This system should protect speech rights from the potential abuses of the government and of private, nongovernmental actors. Governments can support this system by ameliorating content distortions in present-day media, providing access to communication facilities, and promoting the widespread availability of information (Emerson, *System of Freedom* 4).

In ignoring the real conditions that shape opportunities for speech, law-makers and policy-makers ignore the myriad ways that commercial media markets distort democratic communication processes. Media economics suggest that competitive, commercial media industries do not always or in-evitably produce an environment conducive to democratic communication. As we have seen, efficient and well-functioning commercial media processes systematically fail to produce a full range of information and entertainment and to register the interests of entire segments of their audience. In many cases, these ignored audiences are disempowered and marginalized social groups—the poor, the elderly, and ethnic minorities—whose opinions and perspectives should be vital to public culture and debate. Empirical analyses of media economics and behavior suggest that policy-makers should not reify the market or assume the benevolence of market forces. Rather, they should recognize markets as socially constructed institutions that can have a range of effects and that they can modify to achieve different results. Given the real conditions under which media operate, First Amendment interpretations that obviate reference to the empirical world and that curtail consideration of policy intervention do a profound disservice to liberal democracies.

Turning a blind eye to the real conditions that affect democratic com-munication also results in inconsistent free-speech policy. Current dispari-ties in the First Amendment media law of print and broadcast are largely the result of a myopic legal vision that fails to consider factors that inhibit speech outside of technical market failure. As Tuchman and others have pointed out, the result is differential regulation of these media forms despite the knowledge that both face little competition and shun radical or contro-versial viewpoints (176). Furthermore, as media converge in form and func-tion, the regulatory disparities between different media become even more pronounced. Yet, the solution to these inconsistencies is not to deregulate all media, as many market advocates suggest. Instead, policy-makers should evaluate the range of factors that inhibit democratic communication and formulate policies that mitigate the negative effects of both governmental and nongovernmental sources of coercion.

Although current interpretations of the First Amendment typically avoid such evaluations, some cases do provide precedent for considering the real conditions under which media operate. Barron has suggested that the social impact of media could serve as a basis for reasonable policy intervention

(*Public Rights* 177). In *FCC v. Pacifica,* the Court expounded the notion that the social impact and "pervasive presence" of broadcasting justifies some regulation of the medium. Although *Pacifica* dealt with rules intended to protect children from indecency, rather than rules designed to foster democratic communication, the case asserts that the role of broadcasting in society is relevant to First Amendment considerations. *Denver Area* recognized that this rationale could also apply to cable television. That is, the social impact of cable television also may warrant some regulation of the medium. *Turner II* likewise argued that broadcast television's essential role in national discourse warranted regulations that curbed the market power of cable operators to jeopardize this competing source of information. *Janet Reno v. ACLU* struck down indecency regulation that would alter the otherwise democratic conditions surrounding Internet communication.

In *Associated Press,* the Court determined that government regulation could prevent private powers from unduly censoring free speech. The case argued that the application of antitrust law to a combination of newspaper publishers whose business practices monopolized and restrained trade did not violate the First Amendment. The Court said:

> It would be strange indeed . . . if the grave concern for freedom of the press which prompted adoption of the First Amendment should be read as a command that the government was without power to protect that freedom. The First Amendment, far from providing an argument against application of the Sherman Act, here provides powerful reasons to the contrary. That Amendment rests on the assumption that the widest possible dissemination of information from diverse and antagonistic sources is essential to the welfare of the public, that a free press is a condition of a free society. Surely a command that the government itself shall not impede the free flow of ideas does not afford non-governmental combinations a refuge if they impose restraints upon that constitutionally guaranteed freedom. Freedom to publish means freedom for all and not for some. Freedom to publish is guaranteed by the Constitution, but freedom to combine and keep others from publishing is not. Freedom of the press from governmental interference under the First Amendment does not sanction repression of that freedom by private interests. (*Associated Press* 20)

The Court did not allow the Associated Press to use the First Amendment in defense of business practices that harmed the public interest in free trade. Additionally, the Court permitted the government to regulate the media in order to preserve the First Amendment value of a diversity of information sources. The courts could use this same rationale to support regulation seeking to mitigate the distorting influences that today's media markets have on speech (Baker, *Advertising* 134).

The Media Have a Public Function

From the vantage of participatory-democratic theory, it is clear that media have a public function and character. Media are deeply implicated in democratic processes. They are instruments of social mediation and key sites for legitimate public-opinion formation. They make it possible for the public to know its own experiences and interests, to develop a conception of the common good, and to make informed decisions about matters requiring collective action. If media are to serve democratic goals and values, law must acknowledge that this public function exists whether a specific media organization is public or private, old or new, or technically or economically scarce. Recognition of the public function of media is a necessary step toward building media systems that can realize and sustain democratic communication. Indeed, judicial adoption of this policy principle would have profound implications for the fate of media regulations invoking public participation and accountability, for the future of public-forum law, and for the legal status of mediated public space.

The history of Supreme Court law shows that justices who recognize media as critical public resources for information and communication support policies that enhance media accountability and public participation. In 1900, the Supreme Court declared that an early communication network, the telegraph, had a quasipublic function, performed a public service, and needed to treat customers equally with respect to service and charges (*Western Union Telegraph v. Call Publishing* 98, 100). In *Red Lion,* the Court determined that because broadcasters controlled public airwaves and were public trustees, they could be held to fairness policies designed to protect the public's speech interests. In his dissent to *CBS v. DNC,* Justice Brennan argued that, since they are the nation's primary source of news and information, broadcasters should provide a public right of access. Citing *Associated Press,* Brennan maintained that the public character of broadcasting was reason enough to protect diversity of information and information sources in the medium. Finally, in his dissent to *Denver Area,* Justice Kennedy reasoned that the public underpinnings of access television channels warranted their protection, even on private cable systems. Likening these channels to public easements on private property, Kennedy said that such forums protect the public's legitimate speech interests. In the dissent in *US v. ALA,* Justice Souter argued that public library Internet access is an important site for receiving information and for the free speech of library patrons. As such, First Amendment law should prevent the government from unnecessarily censoring speech in these sites.

Judicial recognition of the public character of media, as well as of other property essential to democratic processes, is also a key aspect of aligning public-forum law with democratic theory and protecting public space. Public-forum law is supposed to defend the public's speech rights from public and private censors alike. But at present, public-forum law applies only to government property that is open to the public for expressive purposes or that has a long tradition of public use. Public spaces that take shape in new media, such as public-access cable television or Internet e-mail, stand little chance of qualifying as public forums. The legal approach that anchors public-forum law in property distinctions, rather than democratic principles, is inadequate for determining speech rights. As many scholars argue, the real consideration in public-forum law should be whether a given property has an intrinsic public function or character that necessitates broad protection of speech rights (Barron, "Access to the Press" 1669; Emerson, *System of Freedom* 679; Ruggles 74; Tribe 994–95). Early public-forum law and dissents in more recent cases further attest to the usefulness of the public-function principle and provide precedents for the reformation of public-forum law in this direction.

Early public-forum law conceded that a property's function, not its ownership status, determined whether the government had an interest in protecting speech rights there. In *Marsh v. Alabama,* the Court said that the public had speech rights on private property that assumed the functions of a town and business district (502). Despite company ownership of the town at issue in *Marsh,* it functioned for its inhabitants like any other. Private ownership did not justify depriving the town's residents of their First Amendment rights (507–8). In *Amalgamated Food Employees Union Local 590 v. Logan Valley Plaza,* the Court maintained that, as far as First Amendment rights were concerned, a private shopping center was functionally equivalent to a community business district (318). The Court held that the government could not use its trespass laws to prevent people from exercising their speech rights in these functionally public settings (319). Referencing *Marsh,* the *Amalgamated v. Logan Valley* opinion noted, "Ownership does not always mean absolute dominion. The more an owner, for his advantage, opens up his property for use by the public in general, the more do his rights become circumscribed by the statutory and constitutional rights of those who use it" (325). In both cases, the Court endorsed the public's speech rights in private spaces that had replaced more traditional public sites for free speech. Moreover, both cases determined the public's speech rights not on the basis of whether the property in question was publicly or privately owned, but on its public function.

Unfortunately, the Court repudiated the public-function rationale in 1976 in *Hudgens v. NLRB,* thereby disabling an apt tool for evaluating the role of modern media in democratic processes (518). Denying employees the right to picket a store in a private shopping center, *Hudgens* overturned *Amalgamated v. Logan Valley* and constricted the reach and import of *Marsh* (*Hudgens* 516–18, 521–22). Public-forum status, said the *Hudgens* Court, applies to private property that takes on, not just one, but "all the attributes of a town, i.e. residential buildings, streets, a system of sewers, a sewage disposal plant and a 'business block'" (516). In making this argument, *Hudgens* detached public-forum law from the public function of property in order to link it to formal characteristics of property. In a dissent to the case, Justices Marshall and Brennan protested this turn of events and argued that the Court had wrongly denied the public its constitutional rights to speak and assemble:

> The Court adopts the view that *Marsh* has no bearing on this case because the privately owned property in *Marsh* involved all the characteristics of a typical town. But there is nothing in *Marsh* to suggest that its general approach was limited to the particular facts of the case. The underlying concern in *Marsh* was that traditional public channels of communication remain free, regardless of the incidence of ownership. Given that concern, the crucial fact in *Marsh* was that the company owned the traditional forums essential for effective communication; it was immaterial that the company also owned a sewer system and that its property in other respects resembled a town.

> In *Logan Valley* we recognized what the Court today refuses to recognize— that the owner of the modern shopping center complex, by dedicating his property to public use as a business district, to some extent displaces the State from control of historical First Amendment forums, and may acquire a virtual monopoly of places suitable to effective communication. The roadways, parking lots, and walkways of the modern shopping center may be as essential for effective speech as the streets and sidewalks in the municipal or company-owned town. (*Hudgens* 539–40)

Marshall and Brennan argued that the government must protect speech rights on critical sites for communication. Whether the property at issue usurps all the functions of a town is inconsequential. What matters is that communities are able to access effective avenues of communication (*Hudgens* 539). Rather than determine speech rights according to a formalistic view of the relationship between private property and the First Amendment, the Court should consider whether private property assumes a public function. Otherwise, the public's speech rights would increasingly lose ground as formerly public spaces and activities came under private control (*Lloyd v. Tanner* 570; Shiffrin and Choper 421). Marshall suggested further that property assumes a public function when it engenders public consequences, influences the larger community, and evokes a public interest in its dedicated uses. In these cases, the government must regulate even private property for the common good (*Hudgens* 544).

While much of the media in the United States are privately owned, they cannot evade their public role and function. Media, from print and broadcasting to cable television and the Internet, are inescapably bound with democratic processes. Law that attempts to ground speech rights in the public or private status of the media makes a specious argument. As I will elaborate shortly, the media can never be wholly private. Nor are the dividing lines between public and private property set in stone. Property rights are social constructs. Every society configures property rights according to the social values they wish to privilege. Rather than assert an essentialist view of property as the foundation of speech rights, lawmakers must recognize the constructed nature of property rights and the public character of all media properties. Adoption of this principle clears the way for judicial support of democratic communication policies when they are needed and prevents private property designations from being thrown up as a categorical roadblock to democratic reform. This is not to say that the public character of media justifies any and all types of government intervention in the name of speech rights. The law will always have to carefully scrutinize government policies affecting speech. Simply stated, the law cannot turn its back on the public interest under the spurious assumption that property distinctions, rather than public character, are an appropriate principle on which to base speech rights.

Hybrid Regulatory Models Are a Viable Means of Protecting Democratic Communication

Up until now, the courts have answered questions about speech rights in the media by developing discrete regulatory models for different technology. The print model accords absolute speech rights to newspapers and magazines. The broadcast model balances the speech rights of individual television and radio broadcasters against those of the public. The common-carriage model denies speech rights to providers of telephone service who must transmit all messages on a nondiscriminatory basis. Yet, with the convergence of old technologies and the emergence of new, lawmakers and policy-makers can no longer turn to the old regulatory models for easy answers. New technologies and services often combine forms and functions of older media, making it difficult to pigeonhole them into established regulatory categories. A single Internet Web page, for example, might include text, graphics, audio, and video all on the same screen. Consequently, the courts cannot simply analogize this medium to older media for regulatory purposes.

In addition, more recent multichannel media are increasingly capable of performing multiple roles over different channels. With the advent of new technologies, greater bandwidth,[1] and sophisticated compression technology,[2] media systems can convey information to the public over multiple channels or lines. Most cable systems offer at least forty channels (*Broadcasting and Cable Yearbook* xxxiii), while direct-broadcast satellites deliver upward of one hundred and fifty channels to viewers (Parsons and Frieden 149). With digital compression technology, even the traditional single-channel broadcaster is now able to squeeze several standard television channels into its allotted spectrum space. In this multichannel environment, a combination of regulatory models applied to the same medium can balance the speech interests of media owners with those of the broader public in a content-neutral fashion. These hybrid regulatory models can allow owners to act as speakers on some channels, while at the same time reserving other channels on the same system for communication by unaffiliated parties and the public. This reservation of channel space constitutes a structural access regulation that is not triggered by the speech of system operators.

Multichannel media can perform a variety of roles and functions aside from simply speaking on behalf of the media owner. As a case in point, consider the many roles played by cable television, the first broadband medium. Brenner points out that cable engages in activities that are both expressive and nonexpressive (331). Cable operators act as speakers when they produce original programming for distribution, such as news and public-affairs programs on local origination channels. They act as program selectors when they choose program services to carry on their systems. Yet, in this capacity, cable operators have only a weak editorial and expressive role since they do not review the content they receive from selected cable networks in advance.

When they retransmit broadcast channels or relay public-access and leased-access programming, operators act as a distribution technology for others. In this latter role, cable operators are entirely nonexpressive. Internet actors likewise encompass multiple functions, ranging from transmitting information over pipelines and acting as a neutral conduit for messages produced by others to publishing self-produced content and moderating discussions and list services. While the former activities are nonexpressive, the latter involve significant expressive dimensions.

Although the media deal in the circulation of communication, not everything they do should count as protected speech or implicate them as speakers. Legal theorists point out that the First Amendment does not cover all activities that involve speech or expression (Schauer, *Free Speech;* Greenawalt).[3] Rather, the theories or values that inform our understanding of the First Amendment delimit the activities that come under free-speech protection. For Schauer, while commonly invoked First Amendment theories may value communication somewhat differently, communicative activities deserving free-speech protections have three aspects in common. These activities require a communicative intent, a message, and someone who perceives the message (*Free Speech* 98). Beyond these commonalities, the specific activities covered by free speech will turn on whichever underlying theory rules in a particular instance. Rightfully excluded from First Amendment protection are forms of communication unrelated to the philosophical reasons for protecting speech. In the case of freedom of the press, the rationale for strong First Amendment protection stems from the press's role in democracy and in the dissemination of political ideas. Whether media deserve special free-press rights should therefore hinge on whether they fulfill a political role, not whether they engage in activities that make use of communications technology (Schauer, *Free Speech* 109). Schauer's analysis suggests that lawmakers can consider the types of communicative activities that media undertake when determining how to apply speech-rights protections. Thus, for First Amendment purposes, a cable operator's selection of channels to carry is not comparable to an individual's choice to express a view. Whereas the individual knows the message that he or she intends to communicate, the cable operator has no knowledge of the message being transmitted. Indeed, Schauer notes that the cable operator's channel selection activities are a far cry analogically from the activities of an individual speaker or even the editorial functions of newspaper publishers ("Cable Operators" 175–76). The cable operator's choices, which are not simply analogous to speech and have more to do with business considerations, need not invoke the same level of

First Amendment protection we would give to a primary speaker with clear communicative intent.

In the cases of cable and satellite television, the multiplicity of roles assumed represents a regulatory compromise between the interests of media operators and those of the public. While system operators may prefer to function solely as speakers and program selectors, public policy mandates that they also act as distribution services for third parties and the public. Media law sanctions these multiple roles and functions to the extent that the courts have declared the constitutionality of government regulations such as "must carry," leased access, and PEG access in cable. Moreover, regulators have distinguished between at least two distinct services provided by computer networks—a "'dumb' transmission mechanism" that merely transports information and an Internet-access service that processes that information (Oxman 12–13). The distinction between network services that involve carriage, like transmission services, and services that implicate content, such as information provision, has implications both for how the courts decide speech rights and how they choose to structure the conditions surrounding computer networks. In *US v. Western Electric,* a lower court held that the government could prevent telephone companies from providing information services over their networks. The court reasoned that phone companies with monopoly control over "essential facilities" would have the ability and incentive to discriminate against competing information service providers (563). As with cable networks, telephone companies could manipulate the speed, quality, and efficiency of network traffic to favor their own information services and discriminate against competitors. According to the court, allowing Western Electric and others to control both transmission and content constitutes a threat to the First Amendment goal of achieving "the widest possible dissemination of information from diverse and antagonistic sources" (586). The likelihood of anticompetitive conduct on the part of the phone companies justifies a government-regulated separation of information and infrastructure services, of content from carriage. In *AT&T v. City of Portland* (2000), *MediaOne Group v. County of Henrico,* and *Brand X Internet Services v. FCC,* the federal appeals courts recognized that cable Internet operators provided two essentially different services, that of a telecommunication transmission service and an information service. While these decisions did not mandate that the government regulate cable Internet operators according to the different types of service they provided, they did suggest that regulators could treat different aspects of the service according to different regulatory regimes. Although the Supreme Court in *Brand X* allowed a different interpretation of the nature of Internet services to stand, it did not invalidate the legitimacy of these earlier interpretations. The Supreme Court's determination that courts must privilege the interpretations of regulatory agencies does not preclude Congress from applying the more accurate and rational view that the Internet incorporates both telecommunication and information services and should be regulated accordingly.

In a sense, hybrid regulatory models are nothing new. Legislators and lawmakers have regarded cable television as a hybrid medium since the late 1960s, treating the cable operator as a speaker on some channels, a common carrier on leased-access channels, and a public forum for all practical purposes on public-access channels. From the beginning, the rationale behind this treatment has been the conviction that a single party should not control so many channels into the home (U.S. FCC, "CATV First Report" 205). Legislation would keep some channel space free from cable-operator control in order to diversify the sources of information offered over this important medium. More recently, these same priorities resurfaced in the Open Video System (OVS) rules in the 1996 Telecommunications Act. Combining elements of common-carrier and cable regulation, OVS was a hybrid regulatory model that telephone companies wanting to become video programmers could choose to follow. In exchange for being subject to fewer restrictions than cable and common carriers, the act required prospective OVS operators to provide nondiscriminatory access to unaffiliated program providers on up to two-thirds of their channels, while reserving the other one-third for the operators' choice of programs. The rules also mandated that OVS operators honor PEG-access requirements, as well as carriage rules for local and noncommercial educational broadcast stations. OVS aimed to strike a balance between operators' abilities to control programming on their own systems and the ability of unaffiliated third parties and the public to gain access to these systems. Although it ultimately failed as a policy model due to lack of adoption, Congress had hoped that OVS would become the dominant and preferred model for telephone companies seeking to compete with incumbent cable operators in the video programming market (Meyerson 273).

Yet, while the Supreme Court has allowed hybrid regulatory models to stand over the years, it has not been comfortable doing so. As the *Denver Area* case shows, the Court is reluctant to confirm the speech rights of leased and public-access programmers on cable systems. More generally, communications law consistently fails to recognize that various media can perform more than one function. Hence, the Court in *CBS v. DNC* does not distinguish between a limited public right of access to broadcasting and a wholesale conversion of broadcasters into common carriers. No Supreme Court cases directly acknowledge the hybrid potential of multichannel media.

The courts must recognize that multichannel media can and do perform numerous functions and that hybrid regulatory models are an appropriate means of protecting democratic communication over these systems. Democratic communication in contemporary liberal societies stands to benefit from hybrid regulation. Media are a vital aspect of democratic processes, and the government must protect democratic communication on these systems. Furthermore, a true diversity of information sources is possible only when major communication carriers remain independent from the content they carry (Geller; Owen). Media operators, particularly those with multiple-channel capacity, can incorporate elements of common-carrier and public-forum models of regulation into their media systems. Both of these models insulate speakers, on a nondiscriminatory basis, from censorship by both the government and the private media operator. Hybrid regulation allows democratic communication forums to coexist with forums devoted exclusively to media-operator speech, advancing the speech rights of both parties.

Speech Rights and Private Property

Lower court cases dealing with computer networks, including *Comcast Cablevision, Cyber v. AOL, CompuServe v. Cyber,* and *Intel v. Hamidi* (2001), suggest that speech rights and speaker status rest with the owners and operators of proprietary network servers and equipment, not with the end users who communicate over these systems. These private actors may assert absolute control over speech that traverses their private property. *US v. ALA,* the only Supreme Court case that might have addressed the positive speech rights of different Internet actors and how the regulatory structure of the medium influences speech rights there, failed to do so.

Different traditions within democratic theory uphold not only different views of speech rights, but also different views of property rights. Under neoliberalism, property rights, like all other rights, are thought of in defensive terms. That is, property rights work best when the government takes a hands-off approach to property regulation. The neoliberal view of property rights, like its view of speech rights, has its origins in classical liberalism. Classical liberals sought to circumscribe the tyrannical power of monarchs by shielding rights and freedoms from government action. They conceptualized individual freedom as part of a private sphere of action, while state action belonged to a clearly delineated public realm. Property was part of this purely private realm and was seen as a natural or preexisting right that was independent of social and political formations. Property rights continue to hold a special place within this strand of liberalism. For many neoliberals, private property constitutes the original and most potent symbol of the boundaries around individual rights and freedoms (Michelman 1337; Nedelsky 8). It represents a protected sphere of individual action on which the state cannot intrude. Within this tradition, property is a private-ownership right that gives its holders absolute power and authority over their possessions. This defensive view of property compliments and reinforces the defensive approach to speech rights in the media. When neoliberal-minded courts view the media as simply another form of private property, they invoke the power and prerogative of the media owner to exert exclusive control over their property. When combined with a defensive view of speech rights, the courts doubly prohibit the state from interfering with the media. When the prerogatives of property holders or managers are applied to government actors, as in *US v. ALA*, this approach likewise gives government the license to control speech in public space.

Neoliberal constructions of private-property rights often act as roadblocks to policies striving toward democratic communication. Any reconceptualization of speech rights will have to contend with and ultimately reject this approach. Participatory-democratic theory provides the basis for a different understanding of property and its attendant rights and the basis for a different conception of the ideal relation between property and speech rights. This tradition emphasizes that rights are social constructs. Democratic collectivities, acting under the auspices of the state, actively choose to enforce rights that they believe further the collective public interest. Legal Realists in the 1920s and 1930s applied this essentially participatory-democratic insight to the concept of property, arguing that the state creates, defines, and enforces property rights through legal mechanisms (Freeman and Mensch 247; Fried 3; Nedelsky 255). Property law gives shape to the meaning of property. Law allows rights holders the power to use their property in certain ways and to withhold or grant certain uses to others. In this view, property rights are defined through, not against, the state. They are a dynamic configuration of legal entitlements that result from social choices intended to further a particular vision of the public good.

Since participatory-democratic theory views the state as an instrument of its citizens and rights as social constructs, it necessarily rejects the neat division that neoliberalism posits between public and private realms. Rights may need protection from government abuse, but the government, as an agent of the people, determines and protects rights in the first instance. It is government, or public power, that creates the allegedly "private" property system by granting property holders legally enforceable rights to possess, use, and exchange property. While property appears to be part of an inviolable private sphere under neoliberal theory, participatory-democratic theory sees property as inevitably intermingled with the public realm. Property is the product of social choices made by members of the most public of institutions, the state. The recognition that there are no clear lines between what is public or private necessarily repositions the role of the state in protecting rights. The central question is no longer whether the state should intervene in matters related to private property, since property rights implicate the state from the outset. The question becomes, rather, how to structure property rights to allow for the maximum social freedom, including freedom of speech in a democratic society, and the greatest social good.

While the neoliberal tradition tends to reify property, characterizing it as an absolute and unchanging set of rights, participatory-democratic theory harbors a view of rights more in tune with contemporary legal-studies scholarship. In this view, property is a changing bundle of rights and entitlements that governments can modify to achieve diverse public-policy goals.[4] The configuration of property rights can change in accord with changing circumstances and needs (Streeter 207; Boyle 49; and Freedman 36). In practice, legal determinations of property rights depend on how lawmakers evaluate the competing interests at stake, as well as the normative visions of society on which they draw.

Participatory-democratic theory and critical legal studies suggest that governments can shape property rights in a number of ways. Terms of ownership need not include absolute control, but might instead incorporate values more directly aligned with democratic rights and freedoms. Baker begins to rethink property rights along these lines when he argues that certain functions and values associated with property are more or less deserving of constitutional protection ("Property" 741). Baker associates property rights that allow for self-expression, help secure resources necessary to a meaningful life, or protect control over objects related to one's identity with democratic values. These rights deserve the most protection. Property rights that simply allow people to engage in markets or to exercise power over others do not serve democratic aims, and government can modify these rights in order to achieve collective goals without harming liberty. Others argue that government can shape property rights to incorporate democratic values such as equalizing the relative power of different social groups, maintaining democratic public spaces, or allowing all citizens to exercise the prerogatives of citizenship (Boyle 28; Michelman 1324).

When courts base speech rights on whether a medium is public or private, they rely on a false dichotomy. The all-or-nothing approach that accords the broader public full speech rights in certain public realms and no speech rights in the private totalizes media as belonging entirely to one sphere or another. This assumption does not hold true in theory or in practice. Participatory-democratic theory highlights the impossibility of neatly separating public from private action. At the same time, the media themselves serve key roles in the democratic process that endow them with a public function. To make speech-rights determinations based on categories of property is to put the cart before the horse. Rather, democratic values should inform how law structures speech rights in the media, whether publicly or privately operated, as well as understandings of property.

Several cases recognize that private property has public aspects that are subject to government regulation. In *Munn v. Illinois* (126), the Supreme Court held that government could legitimately regulate private property that is touched by a public interest or dedicated to a public use. Such property, said the Court, is not purely private. According to the Court, the government creates property rights through law and can change them, as long as it observes due process (134). In addition, two landmark cases during the New Deal era negated an earlier trend in law that prevented government from regulating property and contract in the public interest. In *Nebbia v. New York,* the Court allowed states to fix prices because, as it noted, property rights are not absolute (523). States can regulate private property in order to serve the public good, including its safety, happiness, prosperity, and general welfare (524). Moreover, all property use that has public consequences or affects the broader community gives the public an interest in its use and can be subject to regulation if conditions warrant (533). *West Coast Hotel v. Parrish* overturned earlier precedent and upheld the government's ability to set minimum wage laws. This case argued that the liberty to do as one likes or to make contracts is subject to reasonable regulations designed to protect community interests (392). Liberty, argued the Court, requires that the government protect people from social evils and exploitation that threatens their health, safety, and overall welfare (391). These cases signaled the end of an era where the government's ability to regulate property in the public interest took a backseat to the rights of property holders to be left alone. *Pruneyard Shopping Center v. Robins* upheld the ability of states to protect their residents' free-speech rights in privately owned shopping centers that open themselves up to the public.[5] According to the California Supreme Court, shopping centers invite thousands of people to their premises daily and thus do not have the same privacy or property rights as individuals or small businesses. Deferring to California's interpretation of speech rights as laid out in the state's own Constitution, the U.S. Supreme Court argued that allowing the public to speak in these settings did not violate the owner's property rights to exclude others or constitute an unconstitutional "taking" of their property (*Pruneyard* 83–84). Justice Kennedy's dissent in *Denver Area* also suggests that property law is not indifferent to the social claims put forth by the government on behalf of the public. If the government can reserve rights-of-way for the public on private land, the government can plausibly apply the same logic to public-access channels on privately held media.

Protecting democratic communication in U.S. media involves not only a rethinking of speech rights, but a reconceptualization of property as well. As it does with speech rights, participatory-democratic theory provides a basis for reformulating property rights along more empowering lines. Without an empowering conception of the relationship between property and free speech, there is little hope of creating opportunities for participatory communication on otherwise privately owned and managed media.

Conclusion

Felix Cohen, a seminal figure in Legal Realism, has said that there are only two significant questions in law: how the courts actually decide cases, and how they should decide cases (Cohen 824). This book accepts that premise. If ideas about how democracy should function set the parameters for how courts decide First Amendment law, First Amendment law in turn determines the boundaries of democratic communication. How the courts decide cases makes some actions possible and precludes others. Anyone concerned with the future of democratic communication should pay attention to developments in media law and advocate a view of the First Amendment that is consistent with democratic goals and values. Ultimately, First Amendment law will define the baseline terms and conditions under which all citizens can exercise free speech.

The defensive approach to First Amendment law, coupled with defensive notions of property rights, is often inimical to democratic communication. In a communication environment dominated by private media companies, this approach leaves the vast majority of citizens with no right to speak in the prevalent forums of discussion and debate. Neither widespread deregulation nor the development of new, multimedia technologies offers a remedy for the shortcomings of this approach. Deregulation aims to allow the market to settle disputes over media resources without regard for considerations of equity, openness, and social interaction, and even the most promising of new technologies will find it difficult, if not impossible, to maintain a democratic character against the onslaught of market pressures and proposed laws that threaten to alter their technologies, practices, and structures. Rather, as I argue throughout this book, the realization of democratic communication requires a different approach to understanding speech rights.

Participatory-democratic theory, with its empowering view of speech rights, presents an alternative vision of the meaning of democratic communication within political liberalism. Participatory theory offers law and policy advocates a coherent framework for comprehending the role of communication in democratic processes and the conditions necessary for such communication. The empowering approach to speech rights outlined in this book suggests an alternative set of principles to apply to communication law and policy and provides a genuine means of closing the gap that currently exists between First Amendment interpretations and democratic communication.

Although the defensive approach has dominated legal, and to some extent popular, ideas about speech rights in the media, the possibility of a change in thinking persists. Longstanding debates over the meaning and interpretation of the First Amendment demonstrate that law is not set in stone, but is a dynamic and flexible instrument capable of responding to new developments and insights on the nature of political and economic life. Indeed, the malleable nature of law can facilitate momentous transformations in legal thought. Recall, for example, developments in First Amendment law in the 1930s that resulted in the extension of speech rights to all speakers on public property. Free-speech advocates, including policy-makers, scholars, media activists, and ordinary citizens, could well argue that the First Amendment is overdue for another such transformation—this time with respect to modern electronic media.

The ongoing ability of the Internet, and any other new technologies, to sustain democratic communication depends on whether these forums can provide access to a broad base of citizens and can continue to host a wide range of speech from diverse sources. Uncritical celebrants of the Internet claim that the very structure of the technology, with its multiple points of access, interactive capabilities, and decentralized message paths, inherently and irrevocably favors democratic communication. Yet, both media history and current developments in Internet law, policy, and practice suggest that this is not the case. As history shows, technological capabilities alone do not determine the shape and structure of media. In the 1920s, for example, ham radio operators routinely broadcast messages over the public airwaves using inexpensive, often homemade, radio transmitters. While the technology of radio accommodated multiple points of access and a high degree of interactivity, the federal government quickly opted for a model of broadcasting that allowed private interests to capitalize on the rationing of broadcast resources. Licensing the majority of spectrum space to commercial broadcasters, the government facilitated a change in radio's structure that favored some of radio's technological capabilities but inhibited others. Widespread speech opportunities faded as radio became the province of commercial license holders. Private-sector interest in the Internet as a tool for business and trade and government attempts to control objectionable speech online may also precipitate changes in the structure of computer networks. Rising social conflicts over access, pornography, indecency, and obscenity have spurred numerous legal cases asking the courts to expedite control over Internet communication. Whether commercial actors, government interests, or legal decisions affect the structure of the Internet or refashion it in ways that are more profitable and palatable, though less open, remains to be seen. What is certain, however, is that First Amendment interpretations will help determine the degree to which democratic communication survives and thrives on this new medium.

Legal interpretations of First Amendment law alone cannot guarantee a future where democratic communication and democratic processes reign. Other factors—economic, political, and social—may also condition the range and scope of democratic practices. Yet, good First Amendment law does provide an indispensable foundation for democratic communication. Without it, there is no basis on which to build the resources, structures, institutions, practices, and processes that facilitate democratic communication. Consequently, critical analysis of the current state of First Amendment law is a necessary starting point for reviving democratic communication in U.S. media, and empowering speech rights offer an apt base for supporting the communication needs of democratic societies.

NOTES

Chapter 1: The First Amendment and Communication in Democratic Societies

1. Kairys notes that the labor movement began fighting for free-speech rights in the 1870s (246). Labor groups thought that speech rights were a necessary component of the right to organize.

2. See *Nebbia v. New York* and *West Coast Hotel v. Parrish.*

3. In his later work, Meiklejohn recognized that speech having to do with culture and the arts also plays a role in democratic processes (*Political Freedom*).

4. Whether markets or governments structure communication resources, both regulate in the sense that they create written and unwritten rules and constraints that govern behavior with respect to these resources.

Chapter 2: Rethinking Speech Rights

1. For this reason, McQuail holds that this theory is better classified according to the principles for which it stands, rather than by its diverse theoretical roots (121–23). He counts among these principles a right to communication or a right of media access for individual citizens; the need for media forums that are relatively autonomous from both state and market control; media that serve the interests of audiences rather than media corporations, professionals, or clients; the provision of local community media; and the preferences for small-scale, interactive, and participatory media over large-scale, one-way, and professionalized media.

2. Hayek objects to government interference that impairs market processes or formulates alternative schemes for the equitable distribution of resources and goods (*Constitution of Liberty* 232). He argues that this type of planning inevitably leads to totalitarianism and the dissipation of economic progress. Yet, Hayek qualifies his rejection of government interference by acknowledging that when private interests

conflict with social welfare, government intervention may be justified (Hayek, *Road to Serfdom* 120–22). Planning that ameliorates insecurities caused by the lack of food, shelter, clothing, and health and other hardships that impair a person's capacity to work is a legitimate instance of state action. Planning does not threaten liberty as long as the advantages imposed are greater than the social costs, regulations are applied across the board, and competition is not distorted. Friedman, on the other hand, is more typical of today's neoliberals in promoting laissez-faire policies except in areas where technical and certain other types of market failure occurs. Technical monopolies, along with negative externalities like pollution, may occasion government regulation to correct market imperfections, but the state should not set a minimum wage, support social security programs, or subsidize public housing (Friedman 27–28).

3. As a utilitarian, however, Mill rejected the notion of natural rights.

4. Though utilitarian, Mill's political theory went beyond utilitarian liberalism in important ways. Utilitarians asserted a general alignment between individual self-interest and the public interest, a belief that individuals should be allowed to pursue their own utility with minimum state intervention, and a conviction that democracy was the best means of making government accountable to the public. Many scholars credit Mill with imparting a moral vision to democratic liberalism that centered on its potential contribution to human development (Held, *Political Theory;* Holden; Macpherson; Roll; Sabine). Mill attempted to revise utilitarian theory by expanding its notion of individual liberties and by justifying limited state action on the grounds of the moral and social development, as well as the utility, of individuals. Though Mill remained a utilitarian in many respects, some of his views would become the foundation for participatory democratic thinking.

5. The work of earlier democratic theorists, like Rousseau and J. S. Mill, also contains elements of participatory-democratic theory. Rousseau believed that political self-rule required direct participation in democratic processes, though he failed to explain how such participation might be achieved on the scale of the nation-state. In a somewhat less radical vein, J. S. Mill contributed to participatory-democratic theory when he argued that government has a role in securing the conditions necessary to human self-development. Participation also played a central role in ancient Greek political philosophy. As Dahl notes, the ancient Greeks believed that democratic polities should be small enough for all citizens to meet together in assemblies, to jointly rule their city, and to personally know one another (16). Since the problems of mediated communication and the terms of liberal discourse are the primary concerns of this book, I limit my discussion to modern liberal participatory-democratic theory.

6. There is an important distinction to be made between audiences and consumers. Audiences use products and services, but do not necessarily pay for them, while consumers pay for the products and services they use (Picard, *Economics and Financing* 102).

7. By audience, I mean a collective measurement of individuals who read, view, listen to, or make use of a specific media product or service.

8. The average newspaper reader is a college graduate, a homeowner, and over the age of 35 and earns more than $40,000 a year (Cranberg, Bezanson, and Soloski 23).

9. Advertisers avoided placing ads on extended television network news programming after the 2001 attacks on the World Trade Center and the Pentagon (Schiesel and Barringer) and during the first Persian Gulf War (Carter).

10. Anthology dramas frequently tackled disturbing social and psychological problems that faced people in everyday life. And as Barnouw points out, when placed next to anthology dramas, commercials that "featured products that solved problems of business and pleasure in a minute or less" seemed fraudulent (106).

11. Gans argues that the more profits are demanded, the less resources are devoted to news coverage (*Democracy and the News*). According to Gans, pressures to manufacture news cheaply, quickly, and efficiently lead to the routinization of news production, which compromises the quality and range of news content.

12. The Herfindahl-Hirschman Index measures the extent of concentration in ownership patterns, as well as in circulation, audience share, and revenues.

Chapter 3: Social Mediation in Print and Broadcast Media

1. For more on the access movement, see Engelman, Berrigan, and Rowland.

2. Since the late 1960s Jerome Barron has advocated a right of access to the press ("Access to the Press"; *Freedom of the Press; Public Rights*). In his article "Legal Foundations of the Right to Know," Thomas Emerson advocates the legal recognition of a right to know.

3. In August 1999, a federal panel ordered the FCC to justify the continued existence of the personal-attack and political-editorializing rules (*Radio Television News Directors Association v. FCC* [1999]; McConnell 13). When the FCC failed to do so, the rules were dropped by order of the court in 2000 (*Radio Television News Directors Association v. FCC* [2000]). The Fairness Doctrine was a casualty of the deregulatory agenda of the FCC in the 1980s. The FCC eliminated the doctrine in 1987 after the Court of Appeals for the District of Columbia decided, in *Meredith v. FCC*, that Congress had never codified the doctrine and that the FCC could repeal it if the agency deemed it no longer in the public interest.

4. The appeals court stated, "The First Amendment values of individual self-fulfillment through expression and individual participation in public debate have long been recognized. We all have an interest in speaking up ourselves as well as in hearing others. It is too late to argue that the First Amendment protects ideas but not an individual's interest in expressing them and doing so in his own way" (*Business Executives' Move for Vietnam Peace v. FCC* 655).

5. Although part of the majority opinion, only three of the seven justices agreed that no state action was present in broadcasting. Two of the justices refrained from deciding this point, believing that it was not relevant to solving the case. Two dissented from this position, arguing that state action was involved.

6. The Florida statute, enacted in 1913, made it a misdemeanor for a newspaper to print an attack on the personal character of a political candidate without offering the candidate an equally prominent space in which to reply (*Miami Herald* 2833).

7. While the Court recounts the arguments of access advocates in three pages, it dismisses them in one paragraph and lays out its rationale for deciding in favor of the *Miami Herald* in two brief pages.

Chapter 4: The Right to Public Space

1. The FCC's 1976 rules required PEG-access channels only on cable systems with upward of 3,500 subscribers. They also allowed operators with limited channel capacity or low demand for access to combine all PEG programming onto one channel (U.S. FCC, "Report and Order on Cable TV" 296–97). Upon revising the rules, one FCC commissioner reflected that the FCC had been oversold the benefits of cable, which had been hawked "as peddlers once sold Lydia Pinkham's Vegetable Compound, a veritable elixir for the ills of our time" (330).

2. At the same time, the 1984 act allowed franchising authorities and cable operators to jointly prohibit illegal or obscene speech through their franchise agreements. Moreover, the act ordered cable operators to provide "lockboxes" to customers who wanted to block obscene or indecent programming (Cable Communications Policy Act of 1984 2801).

3. The *Alliance* court viewed the access requirements as an infringement of cable operators' speech rights. The court said, "The 1984 Act . . . initiated what may be described as a system of private censorship. From 1984 until 1992, Congress gave private parties in charge of programming on public-access channels complete control, free from any operators' oversight, regarding what the cable television audience could see on these channels. During that eight-year period, programmers were the ones exercising control over the content of access programming. In petitioners' terms, they were the ones acting as private censors. When the 1992 Act gave cable operators the option of vetoing decisions of access programmers to televise indecent programs, it simply adjusted editorial authority between two private groups" (*Alliance for Community Media v. FCC* 115).

4. The Court upheld the indecency rules applied to leased-access channels (*Denver Area* 728). Cable operators are federally mandated to reserve leased-access channels for commercial use by parties unaffiliated with the cable operator. Congress devised leased access to promote competition and diversity in cable programming (47 U.S. Code Service §532(b)). Unlike public-access channels, leased-access channels are not intended to promote community or noncommercial expression. Since they do not aim to provide democratic public spaces, they are not especially relevant to this study.

5. Ironically, the Supreme Court ultimately upheld cable must-carry rules, determining that the preservation of free, local broadcast channels and the maintenance of a diversity of information sources were important government interests. See *Turner II*.

6. Thomas states in a footnote that another reason for treating cable television like print media for First Amendment purposes is the competition it faces from new media (*Denver Area* 818 n. 3).

7. The report noted that structural regulations passed muster with the Supreme Court (U.S. Congress: House, *Cable Franchise Policy* 32). In addition, the report thought public-access television rules were less restrictive than cross-ownership rules since the former only denied cable operators from speaking on a few channels while the latter restricted some speakers from having access to an entire medium within certain locales (33).

8. The *CBS* Court said, "Conceivably at some future date Congress or the Commission—or the broadcasters—may devise some kind of limited right of access that

is both practicable and desirable. Indeed, the Commission noted in these proceedings that the advent of cable television will afford increased opportunities for the discussion of public issues" (*CBS v. DNC* 131).

9. The *Hague v. CIO* Court said, "Wherever the title of streets and parks may rest, they have immemorially been held in trust for the use of the public and, time out of mind, have been used for purposes of assembly, communicating thoughts between citizens, and discussing public questions. Such use of the streets and public places has, from ancient times, been a part of the privileges, immunities, rights, and liberties of citizens" (515).

10. For example, *City of Madison Joint School District No. 8 v. Wisconsin Employment Relations Commission* (1976) identifies as public forums open meetings of local public school boards, and *Widmar v. Vincent* (1981) identifies as public forums facilities at public universities that are made available to student groups.

Chapter 5: Democratic Speech Rights on the Internet

1. Standard commercial ISPs have access rates that average about $200 per year. In the United States, there is also a noncommercial, freenet movement that provides free or low-cost Internet service (Wilson).

2. In 1998, 95 percent of Americans had access to at least four local ISPs, and there were six thousand ISPs in existence nationwide (Oxman 17).

3. Although Pool favors market regulation, he recognizes that even in a free market some elements of communication networks may be characterized by bottlenecks, or constricted points on the transmission paths that carry information, and that some industries may remain centralized and monopolistic. As a consequence, he says, a fully competitive communication market might require government-mandated interconnection policies.

4. Sharing this view are Dyson et al.; Litan and Niskanen; Oxman; Werbach; and U.S. White House.

5. At the time of writing, the Supreme Court has decided the constitutionality of the CDA and CIPA, but has twice remanded COPA back to the lower courts for further litigation. See *Ashcroft v. American Civil Liberties Union*.

6. *Renton* held that the zoning ordinance was constitutional because it had not tried to ban the content of adult films from the neighborhood, but rather their secondary consequences, such as increased crime and reduced property values.

7. Another dissent in the case, by Justice Stevens, argued only that the libraries themselves should have the discretion to decide whether to block objectionable materials online (*US v. ALA* 242–48).

8. I use the term "end users" to denote individual participants on the Internet, not ISPs who interconnect with the core infrastructure.

9. Modern trespass to chattels law applies to the destruction or intentional interference with chattels, or someone's movable property. Trespass to chattels is actionable only if someone has intentionally dispossessed another of their property. Mere interference with chattels is actionable only if the plaintiff can demonstrate actual damages in the form of physical damage to the property or its loss of use over an extended time period (Christie et al. 60).

10. The court also worried that an expanded trespass to chattels law would make

a trespass of unsolicited phone calls and faxes, as well as unwanted radio and television broadcasts (*Intel* 46).

11. The FCC defines broadband as the capability to send information through the network at a speed of at least 200 kbps both upstream and downstream (U.S. FCC, "Deployment of Advanced Telecommunications").

12. Regulated in part by municipal franchise authorities, many cable operators faced open-access rules as a condition of franchise transfers. Communities that mandated open access included Portland, Oregon; Broward County, Florida; San Francisco, California; and Fairfax City, Virginia (Lathen 14).

13. Specific examples of these practices can be found in Cooper; Feld 28; Lessig, *Future of Ideas* 156–57: and Stein and Kidd 6. For example, AT&T bars customers from transmitting more than ten minutes of streamed video over its cable Internet service, and AOL prohibits its commercial partners from providing links to sites not affiliated with AOL (Aufderheide, "Walled Gardens" 8). See Cooper for a particularly detailed account of the ways that infrastructure providers can discriminate on their networks.

14. According to the 1996 Telecommunications Act, a "telecommunications carrier" provides telecommunications to the public "regardless of the facilities used" and should be treated as a common carrier (47 U.S. Code §153(44) and (46)). An "information service" offers "a capability for generating, acquiring, storing, transforming, processing, retrieving, utilizing, or making available information via telecommunications" and invokes less stringent regulation (47 U.S. Code §153(20)).

15. Morley and Gelber point out that these private networks are also known as private/public-access networks because of their dependence on public carriers (77).

Chapter 6: The Future of Democratic Communication

1. Bandwidth is a measure of the capacity of communications media. The greater the bandwidth, the more information a communication system can carry over a given time and space.

2. Compression refers to the process of condensing the amount of information needed to transmit video, audio, or data signals. Compression also allows communication systems to carry more information over a given space.

3. Classic examples of speech not covered by the First Amendment include perjury and fraud.

4. Michelman points out that law routinely modifies property rights for a variety of reasons, including to settle conflicts between holders of adjacent property, to mitigate economic market failure, and to serve competing values such as health, safety, and equality (1319–20).

5. The Court acknowledged that states could determine whether to provide additional speech rights for their residents, but did not suggest that the U.S. Constitution required all citizens to have speech rights on private property. It did note, however, that law provides ample precedent for allowing states to restrict private-property rights to exclude others, as long as those restrictions do not constitute a taking without compensation or violate other federal constitutional provisions (*Euclid v. Ambler Realty* and *Young v. American Mini Theatres,* cited in *Pruneyard*).

BIBLIOGRAPHY

Abrams v. United States. 250 U.S. Reports 616. 1919.

Abramson, Jeffrey B., F. Christopher Arterton, and Gary R. Orren. *The Electronic Commonwealth: The Impact of New Media Technologies on Democratic Politics.* New York: Basic Books, 1988.

Albarran, Alan B. *Media Economics: Understanding Markets, Industries, and Concepts.* 2nd edition. Ames: Iowa State University Press, 2002.

Alliance for Community Media v. Federal Communications Commission. 56 Federal Reporter 3d. 115. 1995.

Amalgamated Food Employees Union Local 590 v. Logan Valley Plaza Inc. 391 U.S. Reports 309. 1968.

Ashcroft v. American Civil Liberties Union. 124 Supreme Court Reporter 2783. 2004.

Associated Press v. United States. 326 U.S. Reports 1. 1945.

AT&T Corporation v. City of Portland. 43 Federal Supplement 2d. 1146. D.Or. 1999.

AT&T Corporation v. City of Portland. 216 Federal Reporter 3d. 871. 9th Circuit Court of Appeals. 2000.

Atkin, David, and Barry Litman. (1986). "Network TV Programming: Economics, Audiences, and the Ratings Game, 1971–1986." *Journal of Communication* 36.3 (1986): 32–50.

Aufderheide, Patricia. *Communications Policy and the Public Interest.* New York: Guilford, 1999.

———. "Walled Gardens or Enclosure Movement? The Debate over the Public Interest in the AOL–Time Warner Merger." ICA Conference. Washington, D.C. 25 May 2001.

Aurigi, Alessandro, and Stephen Graham. "The 'Crisis' in the Urban Public Realm." Pages 57–80 in *Cyberspace Divide: Equality, Agency, and Policy in the Information Society.* Edited by Brian D. Loader. New York: Routledge, 1998.

Bagdikian, Ben H. *The Media Monopoly.* 6th edition. Boston: Beacon, 2000.

Baker, C. Edwin. *Advertising and a Democratic Press.* Princeton: Princeton University Press, 1994.

———. "Giving the Audience What It Wants." *Ohio State Law Journal* 58.2 (1997): 311–417.

———. *Human Liberty and Freedom of Speech.* New York: Oxford University Press, 1989.

———. *Media, Markets, and Democracy.* New York: Cambridge University Press, 2002.

———. "Property and Its Relation to Constitutionally Protected Liberty." *University of Pennsylvania Law Review* 134.4 (1986): 741–816.

Barber, Benjamin R. *Strong Democracy: Participatory Politics for a New Age.* Berkeley: University of California Press, 1984.

Barnouw, Erik. *The Sponsor.* New York: Oxford University Press, 1978.

Barron, Jerome A. "Access to the Press—A New First Amendment Right." *Harvard Law Review* 80.8 (1967): 1641–78.

———. *Freedom of the Press for Whom? The Right of Access to Mass Media.* Bloomington: Indiana University Press, 1975.

———. *Public Rights and the Private Press.* Toronto: Butterworth, 1981.

Barron, Jerome A., and C. Thomas Dienes. *First Amendment Law in a Nutshell.* St. Paul: West, 1993.

Behlendorf, Brian. "Open Source as a Business Strategy." Pages 149–70 in *Opensources: Voices from the Open Source Revolution.* Edited by Chris DiBona, Sam Ockman, and Mark Stone. Cambridge: O'Reilly, 1999.

Benkler, Yochai. "Net Regulation: Taking Stock and Looking Forward." *University of Colorado Law Review* 71 (2000): 1203–61.

———. "Property, Commons, and the First Amendment: Towards a Core Common Infrastructure." March 2001. White Paper for the First Amendment Program, Brennan Center for Justice at New York University Law School. http://www.benkler.org/WhitePaper.pdf (accessed 31 Dec. 2005).

Benton Foundation. "The Telecommunications Act of 1996 and the Changing Communications Landscape." 1996. http://www.benton.org/publibrary/policy/96act/home.html (accessed 15 Oct. 2004).

Berkshire Cablevision of Rhode Island v. Burke. 773 Federal Reporter 2d. 382. 1st Circuit Court of Appeals. 1985.

Berrigan, Frances J., ed. *Access: Some Western Models of Community Media.* Paris: UNESCO, 1977.

Bettig, Ronald V., and Jeanne Lynn Hall. *Big Media, Big Money.* Lanham, Md.: Rowman & Littlefield, 2003.

Blum, Alan. "The Marlboro Grand Prix: Circumvention of the Television Ban on Tobacco Advertising." *New England Journal of Medicine* 324 (1991): 913–17.

Bobbio, Norberto. *The Future of Democracy: A Defense of the Rules of the Game.* Cambridge: Polity Press, 1987.

Bolger v. Youngs Drug Products Corp. 463 U.S. Reports 60. 1983.

Boyle, James. *Shamans, Software, and Spleens: Law and the Construction of the Information Society.* Cambridge: Harvard University Press, 1996.

Brand X Internet Services v. Federal Communications Commission. 345 Federal Reporter 3d. 1120. 9th Circuit Court of Appeals. 2003.

Brenner, Daniel L. "Cable Television and Freedom of Expression." *Duke Law Journal* 223 (1988): 329–88.

Brenner, Daniel L., and Monroe E. Price. *Cable Television and Other Nonbroadcast Video.* New York: Clark Boardman Callagham, 2002.

Brief for Appellee Pat L. Tornillo Jr., No. 73-797. 1973, October Term. Filed with the Supreme Court of the United States in *Miami Herald Publishing Company v. Tornillo.*

Broadcasting and Cable Yearbook 2003/2004. "Year in Review 2002." New Providence: Bowker, 2003.

Burton v. Wilmington Parking Authority. 365 U.S. Reports 715. 1961.

Business Executives' Move for Vietnam Peace. 25 *FCC Reports* 2d. 242. 1970.

Business Executives' Move for Vietnam Peace v. Federal Communications Commission. 450 Federal Reporter 2d. 642. D.C. Circuit Court of Appeals. 1971.

Cable Communications Policy Act of 1984. Pub. L. 98-549. 30 Oct. 1984. 98 Stat. 2779.

Cable Television Consumer Protection and Competition Act of 1992. Pub. L. 102-385. 5 Oct. 1992. 106 Stat. 1460.

Calabrese, Andrew, and Mark Borchert. "Prospects for Electronic Democracy in the United States: Rethinking Communication and Social Policy." *Media, Culture, Society* 18.2 (1996): 249–68.

Carey, James W. *Communication as Culture: Essays on Media and Society.* Boston: Unwin Hyman, 1988.

Carter, Bill. "Many Sponsors Avoiding TV War Reports: Companies Fear Their Upbeat Ads Will Run Alongside Tragic News." *New York Times* 7 Feb. 1991: D1.

Cate, Fred H. "The First Amendment and the National Information Infrastructure." *Wake Forest Law Review* 30.1 (1995): 1–50.

Cauley, Leslie. "Telecom Czar Frets over New Industry Rules." *Wall Street Journal* 12 Feb. 1996: B5.

Century Federal Inc. v. City of Palo Alto. 648 Federal Supplement 1465. N.D. Cal. 1986.

Child Online Protection Act (COPA). Pub. L. 105-277. _1401. 21 Oct. 1988. 112 Stat. 2681-2736. Codified at 47 USCS _231. 2004.

Children's Internet Protection Act (CIPA). Pub. L. 106-554. _1(a)(4). 21 Dec. 2000. 114 Stat. 2763. Codified at 20 USCS _9134(f) (2004), 47 USCS _254(h)(5) (2004).

Christie, George C., et al. *Cases and Materials on the Law of Torts.* 4th edition. St. Paul: West, 2004.

City of Madison Joint School District No. 8 v. Wisconsin Employment Relations Commission. 429 U.S. Reports 167. 1976.

Civil Rights Forum on Communications Policy. "When Being No. 1 Is Not Enough: The Impact of Advertising Practices on Minority-Owned and Minority-Formatted Broadcast Stations." 1999. http://www.fcc.gov/Bureaus/Mass_Media/Informal/ad-study/ (accessed 18 May 2004).

Cohen, Felix. "Transcendental Nonsense and the Functionalist Approach." *Columbia Law Review* 35.6 (1935): 809–49.

Colby, Dean. "Conceptualizing the 'Digital Divide': Closing the 'Gap' by Creating a Postmodern Network That Distributes the Productive Power of Speech." *Communication Law and Policy* 6.1 (2001): 123–73.

Columbia Broadcasting System Inc. v. Democratic National Committee. 412 U.S. Reports 94. 1973.

Comcast Cablevision of Broward v. Broward County. 124 Federal Supplement 2d. 685. S. D. Fla. 2000.

Communications Decency Act (CDA). 104 Pub. L. 104-104. 8 Feb. 1996. 110 Stat. 56.

Compaine, Benjamin M., and Douglas Gomery. *Who Owns the Media? Competition and Concentration in the Mass Media Industry.* 3rd edition. Mahwah, N.J.: Erlbaum, 2000.

CompuServe Inc. v. Cyber Promotions. 962 Federal Supplement 1015. S.D. Ohio. 1997.

Cooper, Mark. "Open Access to the Broadband Internet: Technical and Economic Discrimination in Closed Proprietary Networks." *University of Colorado Law Review* 71 (2000): 1011–69.

Cranberg, Gilbert, Randall Bezanson, and John Soloski. *Taking Stock: Journalism and the Publicly Traded Newspaper Company.* Ames: Iowa State University Press, 2001.

Curran, James. "The Impact of Advertising on the British Mass Media." Pages 309–35 in *Media, Culture, and Society.* Edited by Richard Collins et al. Beverly Hills, Calif.: Sage, 1986.

———. "Rethinking the Media as a Public Sphere." Pages 27–57 in *Communication and Citizenship.* Edited by Peter Dahlgren and Colin Sparks. New York: Routledge, 1991.

Cyber Promotions Inc. v. America Online Inc. 948 Federal Supplement 436. E. D. Pa. 1996.

Dahl, Robert Alan. *Democracy and Its Critics.* New Haven: Yale University Press, 1989.

Davis v. Commonwealth of Massachusetts. 167 U.S. Reports 43. 1897.

Democratic National Committee. 25 *FCC Reports* 2d. 216. 1970.

Denver Area Educational Telecommunications Consortium Inc. v. Federal Communications Commission. 518 U.S. Reports 727. 1996.

Dewey, John. *The Public and Its Problems.* 1927. Reprinted Athens: Ohio University Press, 1954.

Dominick, Joseph R., and Millard C. Pearce. "Trends in Network Prime-Time Programming, 1953–1974." *Journal of Communication* 26.1 (1976): 70–80.

Donohue, Thomas R., and Theodore L. Glasser. "Homogeneity in Coverage of Connecticut Newspapers." *Journalism Quarterly* 55.3 (1978): 592–96.

Downing, John. "Computers for Political Change: PeaceNet and Public Data Access." *Journal of Communication* 39.3 (1989): 154–62.

Drushel, Bruce E. "The Telecommunications Act of 1996 and Radio Market Structure." *Journal of Media Economics* 11.3 (1998): 3–20.

Dyson, Esther, George Gilder, George Keyworth, and Alvin Toffler. "Cyberspace and the American Dream: A Magna Carta for the Knowledge Age." Pages 240–56 in *Communications Policy and the Public Interest.* Edited by Patricia Aufderheide. New York: Guilford, 1999.

Emerson, Thomas Irwin. "Legal Foundations of the Right to Know." *Washington University Law Quarterly* 1 (1976): 1–24.

———. *The System of Freedom of Expression.* New York: Random, 1970.

Engelman, Ralph. "The Origins of Public Access Cable Television, 1966–1972." *Journalism Monographs* 123 (1990).

Entman, Robert M. *Democracy without Citizens.* New York: Oxford University Press, 1989.

Entman, Robert M., and Steven S. Wildman. "Reconciling Economic and Non-Economic Perspective on Media Policy: Transcending the 'Marketplace of Ideas.'" *Journal of Communication* 42.1 (1992): 5–19.

Enzensberger, Hans Magnus. *The Consciousness Industry.* New York: Seabury, 1974.

Erie Telecommunications Inc. v. City of Erie. 853 Federal Reporter 2d. 1084. 3rd Circuit Court of Appeals. 1988.

Euclid v. Ambler Realty Co. 272 U.S. Reports 365. 1926.

Federal Communications Commission v. Midwest Video Corporation. 440 U.S. Reports 689. 1979.

Federal Communications Commission v. Pacifica Foundation. 438 U.S. Reports 726. 1978.

Feld, Harold. "Whose Line Is It Anyway? The First Amendment and Cable Open Access." *Commlaw Conspectus* 8 (2000): 23–41.

Fiss, Owen M. "Free Speech and Social Structure." *Iowa Law Review* 71.5 (1986): 405–25.

Fowler, Mark S., and Daniel L. Brenner. "A Marketplace Approach to Broadcast Regulation." *Texas Law Review* 60 (1982): 207–57.

Fox, Elizabeth, et al. *Comunicación y Democracia en América Latina.* Lima: Desco, 1982.

Fraser, Nancy. "Rethinking the Public Sphere: A Contribution to the Critique of Actually Existing Democracy." Pages 109–42 in *Habermas and the Public Sphere.* Edited by Craig Calhoun. Cambridge: MIT Press, 1999.

Freedman, Warren. *Freedom of Speech on Private Property.* New York: Quorum, 1988.

Freeman, Alan, and Elizabelth Mensch. "The Public-Private Distinction in American Law and Life." *Buffalo Law Review* 36.2 (1987): 237–57.

Fried, Barbara H. *The Progressive Assault on Laissez Faire: Robert Hale and the First Law and Economics Movement.* Cambridge: Harvard University Press, 1998.

Friedman, Milton. *Capitalism and Freedom.* Chicago: University of Chicago Press, 1962.

Gans, Herbert J. *Deciding What's News.* New York: Pantheon, 1979.

———. *Democracy and the News.* New York: Oxford University Press, 2003.

Garnham, Nicholas. "Amartya Sen's 'Capabilities' Approach to the Evaluation of Welfare: Its Application to Communications." Pages 113–24 in *Communication, Citizenship, and Social Policy: Rethinking the Limits of the Welfare State.* Edited by Andrew Calabrese and J. C. Burgelman. Lanham, Md.: Rowman & Littlefield, 1999.

———. *Capitalism and Communication.* London: Sage, 1990.

Geller, Henry. *Fiber Optics: An Opportunity for a New Policy?* Washington: Annenberg Washington Program, 1991.

Gerbner, George. "Cultural Indicators—the Third Voice." Pages 553–73 in *Commu-*

nication Technology and Social Policy. Edited by George Gerbner, Larry P. Gross, and William H. Melody. New York: Wiley, 1973.

Gillmor, Donald M., Jerome A. Barron, and Todd F. Simon. *Mass Communication Law: Cases and Comment.* 6th edition. Belmont: Wadsworth, 1988.

Gitlin, Todd. *Inside Prime Time.* Berkeley: University of California Press, 2000.

Gitlow v. New York. 268 U.S. Reports 652. 1925.

Goldberg, Marvin E., and Gerald J. Gorn. "Happy and Sad TV Programs: How They Affect Reactions to Commercials." *Journal of Consumer Research* 14.3 (1987): 387–403.

Golding, Peter, and Sue Middleton. *Images of Welfare: Press and Public Attitudes to Poverty.* Oxford: Robertson, 1982.

Gomery, Douglas. "Interpreting Media Ownership." Pages 507–35 in *Who Owns the Media? Competition and Concentration in the Mass Media Industry.* Edited by Benjamin Compaine and Douglas Gomery. 3rd edition. Mahwah, N.J.: Erlbaum, 2000.

Graber, Doris A. *Mass Media and American Politics.* Washington, D.C.: Congressional Quarterly Press, 1984.

Green, Thomas Hill. *Lectures on the Principals of Political Obligation.* 1879–80. Ann Arbor: University of Michigan Press, 1967.

———. "Liberal Legislation and Freedom of Contract." 1881. Pages 21–32 in *Liberty.* Edited by D. Miller. New York: Oxford University Press, 1991.

Greenawalt, Kent. *Speech, Crime, and the Uses of Language.* New York: Oxford University Press, 1989.

Greenhouse, Linda. "High Court Splits on Indecency Law Covering Cable TV." *New York Times* 19 June 1996: 1.

Greer v. Spock. 424 U.S. Reports 828. 1976.

Grotta, Gerald Lou. *Changes in the Ownership Structure of Daily Newspapers and Selected Performance Characteristics, 1960–68.* Diss. Southern Illinois University, 1970. Ann Arbor: UMI, 1970. AAT 7102376.

Habermas, Jeurgen. *The Structural Transformation of the Public Sphere: An Inquiry into a Category of Bourgeois Society.* 1962. Cambridge: MIT Press, 1991.

Hagen, Ingunn. "Democratic Communication: Media and Social Participation." Pages 16–27 in *Democratic Communications in the Information Age.* Edited by Janet Wasko and Vincent Mosco. Norwood, N.J.: Ablex, 1992.

Hague v. CIO. 307 U.S. Reports 496. 1939.

Hart, Jeffrey A., Robert R. Reed, and Francois Bar. "The Building of the Internet: Implications for the Future of Broadband Networks." *Telecommunications Policy* 16.8 (1992): 666–89.

Hayek, Friedrich August. *The Constitution of Liberty.* London: Routledge & Kegan Paul, 1960.

———. *The Road to Serfdom.* 1944. Chicago: University of Chicago Press, 1962.

Hearn, Ted. "FCC Liberates DSL in Parity Bid." *Multichannel News* 8 Aug. 2005: 4.

Held, David. *Models of Democracy.* Stanford: Stanford University Press, 1987.

———. *Political Theory and the Modern State: Essays in Sate, Power, and Democracy.* Oxford: Polity Press, 1989.

Hilton, George W. "The Basic Behavior of Regulatory Commissions." *American Economic Review* 62.2 (1972): 47–54.

Hirsch, Fred, and D. Gordon. *Newspaper Money.* London: Hutchinson, 1975.

Holden, Barry. *Understanding Liberal Democracy.* New York: Allan, 1988.

Hopkins, W. Wat. "The Supreme Court Defines the Marketplace of Ideas." *Journalism and Mass Communication Quarterly* 73.1 (1996): 40–52.

Hops, Jeffrey S. "Content and Control of Public Access Channels on Cable Television after Denver Area Educational Telecommunications Consortium v. FCC: The Non-Forum Forum." *Media Law and Policy* 1997: 15–22.

Horwitz, Robert B. "The First Amendment Meets Some New Technologies: Broadcasting, Common Carriers, and Free Speech in the 1990s." *Theory and Society* 20 (1991): 21–72.

Hudgens v. National Labor Relations Board. 424 U.S. Reports 507. 1976.

Ingber, Stanley. "The Marketplace of Ideas: A Legitimizing Myth." *Duke Law Journal* 1984.1 (1984): 1–91.

Intel Corporation v. Hamidi. 114 California Reporter 2d. 244. Cal. App. 3 Dist. 2001.

Intel Corporation v. Hamidi. 1 California Reporter 3d. 32. Cal. 2003.

International Society for Krishna Consciousness Inc. v. Lee. 505 U.S. Reports 672. 1992.

Iyengar, Shanto, and Donald R. Kinder. *News That Matters.* Chicago: University of Chicago Press, 1982.

Jakubowicz, Karol. "Civil Society, Independent Public Sphere, and Information Society: An Impossible Combination?" Pages 78–102 in *Information Society and Civil Society: Contemporary Perspectives on the Changing World Order.* Edited by Slavko Splichal et al. West Lafayette: Purdue University Press, 1994.

Janet Reno v. American Civil Liberties Union. 521 U.S. Reports 844. 1997.

Kairys, David. "Freedom of Speech." Pages 237–72 in *The Politics of Law: A Progressive Critique.* Edited by David Kairys. New York: Pantheon, 1990.

Kalita, Jukti Kumar, and Robert H. Ducoffe. "A Simultaneous-Equation Analysis of Pricing, Circulation, and Advertising Revenue for Leading Consumer Magazines." *Journal of Media Economics* 8.4 (1995): 1–16.

Keane, John. *The Media and Democracy.* London: Polity Press, 1991.

Kellner, Douglas. *Television and the Crisis of Democracy.* San Francisco: Westview, 1990.

Koschat, Martin, and William P. Putsis. "Who Wants You When You're Old and Poor? Exploring the Economics of Media Pricing." *Journal of Media Economics* 13.4 (2000): 215–32.

Kraus, Sidney, and Dennis Davis. *The Effects of Mass Communication on Political Behavior.* University Park: Pennsylvania State University Press, 1976.

Krim, Jonathan. "Cable Firms Faulted for Restrictions on Internet Service." *Washington Post* 28 June 2002: E3.

Labunski, Richard. "The First Amendment at the Crossroads: Free Expression and New Media Technology." *Communication Law and Policy* 2.2 (1997): 165–212.

Lacy, Stephen. "Content of Joint Operation Newspapers." Pages 147–60 in *Press Con-*

centration and Monopoly: New Perspectives on Newspaper Ownership and Opera-tion. Edited by Robert G. Picard et al. Norwood, N.J.: Ablex, 1988.

Lathen, Deborah H. *Broadband Today.* FCC Cable Services Bureau Staff Report, Oct. 1999. http://www.fcc.gov/Bureaus/Cable/Reports/index2.html (accessed 12 Oct. 2004).

Lessig, Lawrence. *Code and Other Laws of Cyberspace.* New York: Basic Books, 1999.
———. *The Future of Ideas: The Fate of the Commons in a Connected World.* New York: Random, 2001.

Lipschultz, Jeremy Harris. *Free Expression in the Age of the Internet.* Boulder: West-view, 2000.

Litan, Robert E., and William A. Niskanen. *Going Digital!* Washington, D.C.: Brook-ings Institution and Cato Institute, 1998.

Lloyd Corp. v. Tanner. 407 U.S. Reports 551. 1972.

Locke, John. "Second Treatise on Government." 1688. Pages 243–79 in *Princeton Readings in Political Thought.* Edited by Mitchell Cohen and Nicole Fermon. New Jersey: Princeton University Press, 1996.

MacCallum, Gerald C. "Negative and Positive Freedom." 1967. Pages 100–122 in *Lib-erty.* Edited by David Miller. New York: Oxford University Press, 1991.

Macpherson, Crawford Braugh. *The Life and Times of Liberal Democracy.* Oxford: Oxford University Press, 1977.

Marsh v. Alabama. 326 U.S. Reports 501. 1946.

Marshall, Thomas Humphrey. *Citizenship and Social Class,* pages 3–51. 1950. Edited by Thomas Humphrey Marshall and Tom Bottomore. Concord, Mass.: Pluto, 1992.

McChesney, Robert W. "The Internet and U.S. Communication Policy-Making in Historical and Critical Perspective." *Journal of Communication* 46.1 (1996): 98–124.

McConnell, Chris. "Supreme Court Raises Questions, Offers Few Answers, Cable Television Indecency Rules." *Broadcasting and Cable* 8 July 1996: 21.

McQuail, Denis. *Mass Communication Theory.* 2nd edition. Beverly Hills, Calif.: Sage, 1990.

MediaOne Group Inc. v. County of Henrico. 257 Federal Reporter 3d. 356. 4th Cir-cuit Court of Appeals. 2001.

Meiklejohn, Alexander. *Free Speech and Its Relation to Self-Government.* New York: Harper & Row, 1948.
———. *Political Freedom: The Constitutional Powers of the People.* New York: Oxford University Press, 1965.

Mensch, Elizabeth. "The History of Mainstream Legal Thought." Pages 13–37 in *The Politics of Law: A Progressive Critique.* Edited by David Kairys. New York: Pantheon, 1990.

Meredith Corporation v. Federal Communications Commission. 809 Federal Re-porter 2d. 863. D.C. Circuit Court of Appeals. 1987.

Meyerson, Michael I. "Ideas of the Marketplace: A Guide to the 1996 Telecommuni-cations Act." *Federal Communications Law Journal* 49.2 (1996): 251–88.

Miami Herald Publishing Company v. Tornillo. 418 U.S. Reports 241. 1974.

Michelman, Frank I. "Possession vs. Distribution in the Constitutional Idea of Property." *Iowa Law Review* 72 (1987): 1319–50.

Middleton, Kent R., Bill F. Chamberlin, and Matthew D. Bunker. *The Law of Public Communication.* 4th edition. New York: Longman, 1997.

Mill, John Stuart. *On Liberty.* 1859. New York: Bantam, 1993.

Missouri Knights of the Ku Klux Klan v. Kansas City. 723 Federal Supplement 1347. W.D. Mo. 1989.

Mitchell, William J. *City of Bits: Space, Place, and the Infobahn.* Cambridge: MIT Press, 1995.

Morley, John C., and Stan S. Gelber. *The Emerging Digital Future: An Overview of Broadband and Multimedia Networks.* Danvers, Mass.: Boyd & Fraser, 1996.

Mosco, Vincent. *The Political Economy of Communication: Rethinking and Renewal.* Thousand Oaks, Calif.: Sage, 1996.

Mulgan, Geoff J. *Communication and Control: Networks and the New Economies of Communication.* New York: Guilford, 1991.

Munn v. Illinois. 94 U.S. Reports 113. 1876.

Murdock, Graham. "Large Corporations and the Control of the Communications Industries." Pages 118–49 in *Culture, Society, and the Media.* Edited by Michael Gurevitch et al. London: Methuen, 1982.

Murdock, Graham, and Peter Golding. "Information Poverty and Political Inequality: Citizenship in the Age of Privatized Communications." *Journal of Communication* 39.3 (1989): 180–95.

Napoli, Philip M. *Audience Economics: Media Institutions and the Audience Marketplace.* New York: Columbia University Press, 2003.

———. "The Internet and the Forces of 'Massification.'" *Electronic Journal of Communication* 8.2 (1998). http://www.cios.org/www/ejc/v8n298.htm (accessed 14 Oct. 2004).

———. "The Marketplace of Ideas Metaphor in Communication Regulation." *Journal of Communication* 49.4 (1999): 151–69.

National Cable and Telecommunications Association v. Brand X Internet Services. 125 Supreme Court Reporter 2688. 2005.

Nebbia v. New York. 291 U.S. Reports 502. 1934.

Nedelsky, Jennifer. *Private Property and the Limits of American Constitutionalism.* Chicago: University of Chicago Press, 1990.

"Net Losses?" Editorial. *Los Angeles Times* 10 Aug. 2005, home edition: B12.

Newhagen, John E., and Sheizaf Rafaeli. "Why Communication Researchers Should Study the Internet: A Dialogue." *Journal of Communication* 46.1 (1996): 4–13.

Nixon v. Missouri Municipal League. 124 Supreme Court Reporter 1555; 158 U.S. Supreme Court Reports, Lawyers' Edition 2d. 291 (2004).

Noam, Eli M. "Beyond Liberalization II: The Impending Doom of Common Carriage." *Telecommunications Policy* 18.6 (1994): 435–52.

Nozick, Robert. *Anarchy, State, and Utopia.* New York: Basic Books, 1974.

Owen, Bruce M. *Economics of Freedom of Expression: Media Structure and the First Amendment.* Cambridge: Ballinger, 1975.

Oxman, Jason. *The FCC and the Unregulation of the Internet.* FCC Office of Plans and Policy Working Paper Series 31, July 1999. http://www.fcc.gov/Bureaus/OPP/working_papers/oppwp31.pdf (accessed 12 Oct. 2004).

Pacific Gas & Electric Co. v. Public Utilities Commission of California. 475 U.S. Reports 1. 1986.

Parsons, Patrick. *Cable Television and the First Amendment.* Lexington: Lexington Books, 1987.

Parsons, Patrick R., and Robert M. Frieden. *The Cable and Satellite Television Industries.* Boston: Allyn & Bacon, 1988.

Peters, John D. "John Locke, the Individual, and the Origin of Communication." *Quarterly Journal of Speech* 75.4 (1989): 387–99.

Petty, Richard E., David W. Schumann, Steven A. Richman, and Alan J. Strathman. "Positive Mood and Persuasion: Different Roles for Affect under High- and Low-Elaboration Conditions." *Journal of Personality and Social Psychology* 64.1 (1993): 5–20.

Picard, Robert G. *Media Economics.* Newbury Park, Calif.: Sage, 1989.

———. *The Economics and Financing of Media Companies.* New York: Fordham University Press, 2002.

Picard, Robert G., and Jeffrey H. Brody. *The Newspaper Publishing Industry.* Boston: Allyn & Bacon, 1997.

Pool, Ithiel de Sola. *Technologies of Freedom.* Cambridge: Harvard University Press, 1983.

———. *Technologies without Boundaries: On Telecommunications in a Global Age.* Cambridge: Harvard University Press, 1990.

Posner, Richard A. "Theories of Economic Regulation." *Bell Journal of Economics and Management Science* 5.2 (1974): 335–58.

Post, Robert C. "Between Governance and Management: The History and Theory of the Public Forum." *UCLA Law Review* 34 (1987): 1713–1835.

Pruneyard Shopping Center v. Robins. 447 U.S. Reports 74. 1979.

Quincy Cable TV Inc. v. Federal Communications Commission. 768 Federal Reporter 2d. 1434. D.C. Circuit Court of Appeals. 1985.

Rabinowitz, Victor. "The Radical Tradition in the Law." Pages 426–35 in *The Politics of Law: A Progressive Critique.* Edited by David Kairys. New York: Pantheon, 1990.

Radio Television News Directors Association v. Federal Communications Commission. 184 Federal Reporter 3d. 872. 1999.

Radio Television News Directors Association v. Federal Communications Commission. 229 Federal Reporter 3d. 269. 2000.

Rarick, Galen, and Barrie Hartman. "The Effect of Competition on One Daily Newspaper's Content." *Journalism Quarterly* 43.3 (1966): 459–63.

Red Lion Broadcasting Co. Inc. v. Federal Communications Commission. 395 U.S. Reports 367. 1969.

Renton v. Playtime Theatres Inc. 475 U.S. Reports 41. 1986.

Roberts, Jason. "Public Access: Fortifying the Electronic Soapbox." *Federal Communications Law Journal* 47.1 (1994): 123–52.

Rogers, Robert P., and John R. Woodbury. "Market Structure, Program Diversity, and Radio Audience Size." *Contemporary Economic Policy* 14 (1996): 81–91.

Rogerson, Kenneth S., and G. Dale Thomas. "Internet Regulation Process Model: The Effect of Societies, Communities, and Governments." *Political Communication* 15.4 (1998): 427–44.

Roll, Eric. *A History of Economic Thought.* Boston: Faber & Faber, 1992.

Rorty, Richard. *Consequences of Pragmatism.* Minneapolis: University of Minnesota Press, 1996.

Ross, Chuck. "Marketers to Blame for Lack of Diversity on TV: JWT Report." *Advertising Age* 16 Aug. 1999: 4.

Rousseau, Jean-Jacques. "On the Social Contract." 1762. Pages 280–92 in *Princeton Readings in Political Thought.* Edited by Mitchell Cohen and Nicole Fermon. Princeton: Princeton University Press, 1996.

Rowland, Willard D., Jr. "The Illusion of Fulfillment: The Broadcast Journalism Reform Movement." *Journalism Monographs* 79 (1982).

Rucinski, Dianne. "The Centrality of Reciprocity to Communication and Democracy." *Critical Studies in Mass Communication* 8.2 (1991): 184–94.

Ruggles, Myles Alexander. *The Audience Reflected in the Medium of the Law: A Critique of the Political Economy of Speech Rights in the United States.* Norwood, N.J.: Ablex, 1994.

Sabine, George Holland. *A History of Political Theory.* 4th edition. Hinsdale, Ill.: Dryden, 1973.

Sassen, Saskia. *Globalization and Its Discontents.* New York: New Press, 1998.

Schatz, Amy. "FCC to Seek Parity after Net Ruling." *Wall Street Journal* 29 June 2005: B9.

Schauer, Frederick. "Cable Operators as Editors: Prerogative, Responsibility, and Liability." *Hastings Comm/Ent Law Journal* 17 (1994): 161–78.

———. *Free Speech: A Philosophical Enquiry.* Cambridge: Cambridge University Press, 1982.

Schiesel, Set, and Felicity Barringer. "News Media Risk Big Losses to Cover War." *New York Times* 22 Oct. 2001: C1.

Schiller, Dan. *Digital Capitalism: Networking the Global Market System.* Cambridge: MIT Press, 1999.

Sen, Amartya. *Inequality Reexamined.* Cambridge: Harvard University Press, 1992.

Sheffrin, Steven M. *Markets and Majorities: The Political Economy of Public Policy.* New York: Free Press, 1993.

Shenker, Scott. "Service Models and Pricing Policies for an Integrated Services Internet." Pages 315–37 in *Public Access to the Internet.* Edited by Brian Kahin and James Keller. Cambridge: MIT Press, 1995.

Shiffrin, Steven H. *The First Amendment, Democracy, and Romance.* Cambridge: Harvard University Press, 1990.

Shiffrin, Steven H., and Jesse H. Choper. *The First Amendment: Cases, Comments, Questions.* 2nd edition. St. Paul: West, 1996.

Shoemaker, Pamela J., and Stephen D. Reese. *Mediating the Message: Theories of Influences on Mass Media Content.* White Plains, N.Y.: Longman, 1991.

Smolla, Rodney A. *Free Speech in an Open Society.* New York: Vintage, 1993.

Smythe, Dallas W. "Communications: Blindspot of Western Marxism." *Canadian Journal of Political and Social Theory* 1.3 (1977): 1–27.

Sparks, Colin. "The Press, the Market, and Democracy." *Journal of Communication* 42.1 (1992): 36–51.

Splichal, Slavko. "Searching for New Paradigms: An Introduction." Pages 3–18 in *Communication and Democracy.* Edited by Slavko Splichal and Janet Wasko. Norwood, N.J.: Ablex, 1993.

Stein, Laura. "Access Television and Grassroots Political Communication in the United States." Pages 299–324 in *Radical Media: Rebellious Communication and Social Movements.* Edited by John Downing. Thousand Oaks, Calif.: Sage, 2001.

———. "Democratic 'Talk,' Access Television and Participatory Political Communication." Pages 123–40 in *Community Media in the Information Age: Perspectives and Prospects.* Edited by Nicholas Jankowski and Ole Prehn. Cresskill, N.J.: Hampton, 2002.

Stein, Laura, and Dorothy Kidd. "The Future of Openness on the Internet." *Mediafile* 19.3 (2000): 1, 6–7.

Stein, Laura, and Nikhil Sinha. "Global Media and National Communication Policy." Pages 410–31 in *Handbook of New Media.* Edited by Leah A. Lievrouw and Sonia Livingstone. Thousand Oaks, Calif.: Sage, 2002.

Stigler, George J. "The Theory of Economic Regulation." *Bell Journal of Economics and Management Science* 2.1 (1971): 3–21.

Straubhaar, Joseph D., and Robert LaRose. *Media Now: Communications Media in the Information Age.* Stamford: Wadsworth/Thomson, 2002.

Strauss, Leo. "What Is Political Philosophy?" 1959. Pages 3–57 in *Political Philosophy: Six Essays by Leo Strauss.* Edited by Hilail Gildin. New York: Pegasus, 1975.

Streeter, Thomas. *Selling the Air: A Critique of the Policy of Commercial Broadcasting in the United States.* Chicago: University of Chicago Press, 1996.

"Strike Up the Broadband." Review and Outlook. *Wall Street Journal* 9 Aug. 2005: A10.

Sunstein, Cass R. *Democracy and the Problem of Free Speech.* New York: Free Press, 1993.

Tehranian, Majid. *Technologies of Power: Information Machines and Democratic Prospects.* Norwood, N.J.: Ablex, 1990.

Telecommunications Act of 1996. Pub. L. 104-104. 8 Feb. 1996. 110 Stat. 56.

Thompson, R. Stephen. "Circulation versus Advertiser Appeal in the Newspaper Industry: An Empirical Investigation." *Journal of Industrial Economics* 37.3 (1989): 259–71.

Tribe, Laurence H. *American Constitutional Law.* 2nd edition. Mineola: Foundation, 1988.

Tuchman, Gaye. *Making News: A Study in the Construction of Reality.* New York: Free Press, 1978.

Turner Broadcasting System Inc. v. Federal Communications Commission [= Turner I]. 512 U.S. Reports 367. 1994.

Turner Broadcasting System Inc. v. Federal Communications Commission [= Turner II]. 520 U.S. Reports 180. 1997.

Turow, Joseph. *Breaking Up America: Advertisers and the New Media World.* Chicago: University of Chicago Press, 1997.

———. *Media Industries: The Production of News and Entertainment.* New York: Longman, 1984.

47 U.S. Code. _153(20). 2004.

47 U.S. Code. _153(44) and (46). 2004.

47 U.S. Code Service. _532(b). 2004.

U.S. Congress: House of Representatives. *Cable Franchise Policy and Communications Act of 1984*. House of Representatives Report no. 98-934. 98th Congress, 2d session. Washington: GPO, 1984.

U.S. Congress: House of Representatives. Committee on Energy and Commerce: Subcommittee on Telecommunications and the Internet. Hearing: "Staff Discussion Draft of Legislation to Create a Statutory Framework for Internet Protocol and Broadband Services." http://energycommerce.house.gov/108/Hearings/11092005hearing1706/hearing.htm (accessed 31 Dec. 2005).

U.S. Department of Commerce. *National Information Infrastructure: Agenda for Action*. Washington: GPO, 1993.

U.S. Federal Communications Commission. "Amendment of Section 64.702 of the Commission's Rules and Regulations (Second Computer Inquiry)." *77 FCC Record* 384. 1980.

———. "Appropriate Framework for Broadband Access over Wireline Facilities Policy Statement." *70 FCC Record* 60222. 2005.

———. "Appropriate Framework for Broadband Access to the Internet over Wireline Facilities." *67 Federal Register* 9232. 2002.

———. "Availability of Advanced Telecommunications Capability in the United States." *69 FCC Record* 59595. 2004.

———. "Cable Television Report and Order." *36 FCC Record* 143. 1972.

———. "CATV First Report and Order." *20 FCC Reports* 2d. 201. 1969.

———. "Deployment of Advanced Telecommunications Capability to All Americans in a Reasonable and Timely Fashion." *17 FCC Record* 2844. 2002.

———. "Fairness Doctrine and Public Interest Standards." *39 Federal Register* 26372. 1974.

———. "High-Speed Access to the Internet over Cable and Other Facilities; Internet over Cable Declaratory Ruling." *17 FCC Record* 4798. 2002.

———. "Inquiry concerning High-Speed Access to the Internet over Cable and Other Facilities; Internet over Cable Declaratory Ruling." *67 Federal Register* 18907. 2002.

———. "Notice of Proposed Rulemaking on the Appropriate Framework for Broadband Access to the Internet over Wireline Facilities." *67 Federal Register* 9232. 2002.

———. "Report and Order on Cable TV Capacity and Access Requirements." *59 FCC Record* 294. 1976.

———. "Report on Editorializing by Broadcast Licenses." *13 FCC Record* 1246. 1949.

U.S. White House. *A Framework for Global Electronic Commerce*. Washington: GPO, 1997.

United States v. American Library Association. 156 Supreme Court Reports, Lawyers' Edition 2d. 221. 2003.

United States v. Western Electric Company. 673 Federal Supplement 525. D.C. Circuit Court of Appeals. 1987.

Valdez, Armando. "The Economic Context of U.S. Children's Television: Parameters for Reform?" Pages 145–80 in *Communication and Social Structure: Critical Studies in Mass Media Research.* Edited by Emile G. McAnany, Jorge Schnitman, and Noreene Janus. New York: Praeger, 1981.

Van Alstyne, William W. *Interpretations of the First Amendment.* Durham: Duke University Press, 1984.

Webster, James G., and Patricia F. Phelan. *The Mass Audience: Rediscovering the Dominant Model.* Mahwah, N.J.: Erlbaum, 1997.

Werbach, Kevin. *Digital Tornado: The Internet and Telecommunications Policy.* FCC Office of Plans and Policy Working Paper Series 29, March 1997. http://www.fcc. gov/Bureaus/OPP/working_papers/oppwp29pdf.html (accessed 12 Oct. 2004).

West, Cornel. *The American Evasion of Philosophy: A Genealogy of Pragmatism.* Madison: University of Wisconsin Press, 1989.

West Coast Hotel v. Parrish. 300 U.S. Reports 379. 1937.

Westen, Tracy A. "Barriers to Creativity." *Journal of Communication* 28.2 (1978): 36–50.

Western Union Telegraph Company v. Call Publishing Corporation. 181 U.S. Reports 92. 1901.

Wheeler, Deborah L. "Global Culture or Culture Clash: New Information Technologies in the Islamic World—A View from Kuwait." *Communication Research* 25.4 (1998): 359–76.

Widmar v. Vincent. 454 U.S. Reports 263. 1981.

Wilson, Dave. "Freenets Getting a New Lease on Life." *Los Angeles Times* 20 Dec. 2001: T1.

Young v. American Mini Theatres Inc. 427 U.S. Reports 50. 1976.

Zhao, Yuezhi. "Caught in the Web: The Public Interest and the Battle for Control of China's Information Superhighway." *Info* 2.1 (2000): 41–66.

INDEX

LAURA STEIN is an assistant professor in the Department of Radio-Television-Film at the University of Texas in Austin. Her writing has appeared in numerous journals and books, including *Communication Law and Policy; Media, Culture, and Society; Javnost/The Public; Peace Review; Handbook of New Media; Community Media in the Information Age;* and *Radical Media.* She is currently working on an edited collection entitled *Making Our Media: Global Initiatives toward a Democratic Public Sphere,* about grassroots attempts to transform the policy and practice of information and communication media around the world. She has a B.A. from the University of California at Berkeley, an M.A. in education from Columbia University, and a Ph.D. in communication from the University of Texas in Austin.

The History of Communication

The University of Illinois Press
is a founding member of the
Association of American University Presses.

_____

Composed in 10.5/13 Adobe Minion
at the University of Illinois Press
Manufactured by Thomson-Shore, Inc.

University of Illinois Press
1325 South Oak Street
Champaign, IL 61820-6903
www.press.uillinois.edu